Dear Steve,

I hope you en
wrote this to hope
others to dream big and to
leave a legacy for my father.

It was great to see you and
your family at St. Catherine's
for the gym dedication to your
father!

I consider your Dad as my
first mentor and I will
never forget the individual time
he gave to me to help me become
the best athlete and person at
that time of my life. I'm
forever grateful to him!

My best wishes to you in
the years ahead!

Become your very best!
Far & Sure,
John

YOU CAN BE THE BEST

YOU CAN BE THE BEST

LIFE LESSONS FROM THE BUTCHER AND THE BUSINESSMAN

JOHN PLY

LIONCREST
PUBLISHING

You Can Be the Best

Life Lessons from the Butcher and the Businessman

FIRST EDITION

ISBN 978-1-5445-4020-7 Hardcover
      978-1-5445-4021-4 Paperback
      978-1-5445-4022-1 Ebook
      978-1-5445-4023-8 Audiobook

To my father

If it weren't for you, I wouldn't be writing this book.
The example you set not only for me but for
everyone lucky enough to have known you
truly defines the meaning of success!

CONTENTS

FOREWORD

Author's Note: I always tell people, "When Jack Gleason speaks, you should listen." Jack is a man of few words, and when he chooses to offer his opinions, it's always to share something valuable. So when Jack agreed to write the foreword for me, I was honored.

Success. What is it? How do you define it? Who would you consider successful? Why? And perhaps the most important question of all: How can you be successful?

The following pages provide one person's answers to these questions—a fascinating exploration of what constitutes success, the path that can be taken, and the measurements to confirm success. In this book, John opens his heart to share with the reader personal, and sometimes private, experiences about his and his father's life journeys. The reader gets the opportunity to understand how the very diverse backgrounds of a father and son resulted in the same outcome: extraordinary success in each of their lives, as confirmed by the way they used their success to make the lives of others better. Drawing on the lessons learned from hard-won experience, John lays the groundwork for how anyone can lead a rewarding life, just as he and his father did.

I can definitively make the statement that the stories and lessons from John's life are fascinating because I have had a front-row seat to watch it all unfold. I first met John in first grade and consider him my closest and longest non-family friend. We have persisted as friends together through all the stages of life to follow: our high school, college, family, early, middle, and senior years.

Being friends with John also gave me the chance to know his father. I can't say I knew him well, but I saw, and more importantly sensed, plenty. I considered him a genuinely nice man who never seemed to be concerned about himself, only his family and others. Even in his later years, his smile and kind disposition never faded. You could just sense he was a special person.

John and I are very different, yet when I think through the book's contents, so much alike. Our summer caddying and golf adventures were the best. Seven days a week together, talking, laughing, learning about life. During our formative caddy years, when John and I discussed the future and our goals, I probably had a better sense of where I thought I was going. John may not have had the same sense, but it never worried me. Because with John, you just knew he was going places. He was always a gracious winner in everything he did. It showed in sports—as a football quarterback, basketball captain, standout golfer. It showed through work, in which John was among the best caddies and a scholarship winner. It was evident in everything he did.

With all the hours we have spent together in the six decades we have known each other, I guess I would have recognized early on what his greatest trait was. I think I probably did. Yes, I can see it now as I look back. John has accomplished many things that people would deem to be success. The prestige, money, houses, cars are visible. But what makes John the best is something not seen, but felt: his heart. John cares about giving to others and making life better for others. Not because he looks for validation for himself, but because he really, really cares. It is John's heart that you will find in these pages. It is what makes this book special and what I hope will inspire you to your own greatness.

With that as background, I send you off to read the following pages and the fascinating stories that will help you to define success and learn how to achieve it. Have fun reading.

—Jack Gleason

INTRODUCTION

The Success Formula

I'd like to introduce you to two men: Ziggy and Johnny.

Ziggy—full name Zygmunt Plywaczewski—arrived in America from Poland at the age of thirty, with barely a high school education and no particular trade or skill. He wasn't able to speak much English and took menial, low-wage jobs just to survive. Eventually, he secured a job with Swift and Company as a butcher and meat packer. He got up at 4:30 a.m., worked all day in freezer-like conditions, and then went to a second job as a butcher at a retail meat market. With a wife and five children, he put in twelve- and thirteen-hour days to support his family.

Ziggy Ply never made much money. Some weeks, his family couldn't even afford the *Chicago American* newspaper, which cost only 75 cents per week at the time. But even with five growing kids, his family never went hungry. He received significant discounts on meat from Swift, and at the meat market, he was paid with a combination of $20 in cash and boxes of hamburger patties

1

and other meat items. While his family was poor, they never felt destitute, because they always had enough food, love, and happiness.

Ziggy worked until he was sixty-five. When he retired, basically the only asset to his name was his very modest house. But he never complained. Until the day he passed away at ninety four, he always talked about how blessed he was.

Johnny, meanwhile, achieved something possibly no one else in the world has. He started not one, but two companies from scratch that ultimately became the leaders in their respective industries! That alone is impressive. Most people never even start one business because they're too afraid. Of those who do, 70 percent fail within ten years, according to the Bureau of Labor Statistics. Even more interesting is his reason for starting the second company: to become a customer of his first company. At the time, people thought he was crazy, but the potentially risky move paid off. His second company grew to be so profitable that it eventually became the *only* customer of his first company, replacing 120 clients.

But plenty of people have started multiple successful companies. What's special about Johnny is that he grew his two companies to be the *best* in their field—and he did it in industries that had already been around for thirty to fifty-plus years. That would be like starting a new rideshare service right now and becoming the preferred rideshare company over Uber and Lyft in less than fifteen years, or like creating an internet search engine that ultimately becomes more popular than Google. And he did it *twice*.

With his business success, Johnny has enjoyed many of the material comforts that people often associate with success. He's owned multiple beautiful homes and luxury cars—Mercedes-Benz, Ferrari, and Bentley. He has belonged to some of the most exclusive private golf clubs in the US, such as Chicago Golf, Butler National, and Bighorn. He has been able to buy his wife and himself watches and jewelry, expensive clothing, and they've taken several fabulous vacations through the years!

In addition, over his lifetime, he's been able to donate millions of dollars to organizations and causes he cares about.

Between these two men, who was more successful?

If you're like most people, you will probably say Johnny, in which case I'm flattered. Because I'm Johnny.

But if I were to answer that question, I would say Ziggy is more successful. Ziggy is actually the most successful person I've ever met—and I've met many big-name, accomplished presidents and CEOs, including the heads of Fortune 500 companies who oversee billions of dollars in sales. In fact, were it not for Ziggy, I never would have achieved the levels of success I have. I wouldn't even exist. Because Ziggy is my father.

So why is Ziggy the most successful person I've ever met? To answer that, we must first answer a deeper, all-important question: *What is success?*

WHAT IS SUCCESS?

"What is success?" seems like a simple question to answer, but in my experience, people get it wrong more often than they get it right. Our idea of success has been distorted. Because of this, people waste time and energy chasing the wrong things.

Wherever you are in your life—whether you're thirteen years old, twenty-one, thirty, forty-five, or sixty-five—you need to know two things about success:

1. Success is not about financial wealth.
2. Success is not absolute.

You've probably heard it a million times: money isn't everything. But the reality is that when most of us think about success, the first thing that comes to mind is dollars. Through movies, television, the news, and social media, we've been given this message over and over again: success = financial wealth. But some of the wealthiest people I've met in my life are also some of the most miserable. They have more houses and possessions than true friends, and despite having more than enough money to buy whatever they want, they're not content, and they're not doing as much good in the world as they could. Can you call that success?

The other way our idea of success has been distorted is thinking of it as absolute—all or nothing. Think about the Super Bowl. People are quick to write off the losing team. They failed, and only those who win are seen as successful. But is that really fair? Behind that team's loss are years of hard work, endless practices, grueling training, and previous wins. Just making it to the Super Bowl—heck, just making it into the NFL!—is a huge achievement. How can we not see them as successful, because of one loss? Success isn't about winning or losing. Do you even remember who won the Super Bowl five years ago? How about fifteen years ago? You probably don't know, right? So then why would we use that as our measure of success?

So far I've talked only about what success *isn't*. It's not about money, and it's not about how you stack up compared to others. So now, let's talk about what success *is*.

Success is about total happiness. As Jeff Olson says in *The Slight Edge*, "Success doesn't lead to happiness; it's the other way around." What defines my father as the most successful person I know is the level of appreciation and contentment he felt in his life. He was poor in money but rich in all the things that really matter: faith, family, friends, love, kindness, gratitude. Those are the same reasons I consider myself successful. In the opening, I spoke about my financial gains simply to make a point. I feel successful and wealthy not because of the things I own, but because of the friends and loved ones I've been blessed with. I'm still in touch with friends from college, high school, grade school, and even some friends I met before first grade! My life is filled with love and happiness. That's what true wealth is.

Success is also about accomplishment. It's about achieving your dreams and goals, whatever they may be. Because of this, success is relative. You can't measure how far a person has come without knowing where they started. The starting line is different for everybody, as are the challenges encountered along the way. So of course success will look different for everybody too.

Take my father. He left home in 1937 to join the Polish army, shortly before the start of World War II. In the fall of 1939, just shy of his nineteenth birthday, he was captured by the Germans. For more than five and a half years of his life he was held in a POW camp, witnessing horrors I can't even imagine, not knowing when his next meal would come or even whether he was going to live. Many never made it out of those camps, and those who did carried long-lasting mental and emotional scars with them. For my father to go through that experience and then build the life and family he did in America is almost impossible to comprehend. If you think about the effort involved and where he started compared to where he ended, it's far more impressive than what some of the supposedly more successful people in the world—or even I—have accomplished.

Do you understand better now why Ziggy Ply is the poster child for success?

HOW TO BE THE BEST

After understanding what success is, the next logical question is, "How do I achieve it?" The answer is simple: be the best.

I titled this book *You Can Be the Best*. That's a massive promise, and it's not one I make lightly. I can't guarantee that you *will* be the best, but I do guarantee that you *can* be. Being the best isn't about how you measure up compared to others. It's about reaching your full potential, being the best *you*.

What that looks like will be different for everybody, but the method for achieving it is the same. In these pages I share the life lessons you need to be the best. These lessons are a combination of things that my father passed on to me and that I learned through hard-earned experience. These lessons are what guided my father his entire life and what motivated me to be the best and build my companies and hundreds of amazing friendships.

I'm not writing this book to make money. In fact, 100 percent of proceeds from this book will be donated to various charitable organizations. I'm writing this book to inspire others and help them achieve their own personal success, goals, and happiness. If you're someone who might be struggling and wondering, "How am I ever going to get ahead or achieve my dream?"…this book is for you! If I can motivate just one person to dig themselves out of despair and have a happy, successful life, then this book will be a success to me.

These lessons are the formula for success. It doesn't matter what the goals are, the formula is the formula:

- Become the best.
- Pursue your passion.
- Use all your tools.
- Never give up, no matter what.
- Find a way.
- Be honest and trusting.
- Be kind.
- Be grateful.
- Be generous.
- Do good.

No matter your definition of success, no matter what you hope to accomplish, I believe these lessons will help get you there. Because I've already seen it happen.

I've spent my retirement years mentoring younger people, helping them achieve their goals. One of those people was Lilia Vu. I met Lilia at Shady Canyon Golf Club in Irvine, California. I was there practicing one evening, and Lilia was working on her swing close by. As soon as I saw her hit the ball, I thought, *Holy crap.* I'd never seen a woman hit a golf ball as beautifully as Lilia did. As gorgeous as her swing was, I sensed a sadness in her. When things aren't going well for people, you can sort of see it in their eyes. A person's eyes either sparkle, or they don't, and Lilia's eyes that day were not sparkling.

I'm the kind of person who will engage with strangers, because you just never know what might come from saying hello to someone. So I went over to introduce myself and compliment her on her swing. We got to talking, and I found out she used to play on the UCLA golf team. During her collegiate golf career, she had considerable success, including once winning four consecutive tournaments. By the time she graduated, at just twenty-one years of age, she was ranked the number one female amateur in the world. She was so good she qualified to play in several Ladies Professional Golf Association (LPGA) tournaments.

That's when things took a turn for the worse. Her first year as a professional was certainly not what she had dreamed of. She not only played poorly, but the camaraderie from her college golf days was gone. Quite frankly, some players weren't that friendly towards her. She missed seven of eight cuts, which meant she did not qualify to play the weekend and win any money. She lost her playing privileges on the LPGA and had to start all over the following year to try to get them back. Suffice to say, the entire experience was disheartening.

When I met her, she was finishing up her 2020 season on the Symetra Tour (now called the Epson Tour), a tour which allows players a chance to earn their way back to the LPGA. The top ten money winners for the year on Symetra get a card to play on the LPGA Tour. Unfortunately for Lilia, this season also didn't go well for her, and she already knew she wouldn't be getting her LPGA playing card back that year.

With this background, I understood the sadness in Lilia's eyes, but I also saw her great potential. The very next day I was again practicing next to her at the driving range. We continued our conversation from the previous evening, and I then mentioned to her that if she would be open to it, I felt I could help her achieve her golf goals and more.

Some people might have been hesitant about such an offer, but Lilia was willing to take a chance with me. She quickly said, "Yes, I'd love to!"

Now, golf is a passion of mine, and I've become a decent amateur golfer, but I'm still just an amateur. For Lilia, golf is her career. The first time we actually played golf together, she drove the ball beautifully, her short game was exceptional, and she was the best four-foot putter I'd seen since Tiger Woods. What could I possibly teach a professional-level golfer like her? A lot, it turns out. Because the help she needed most wasn't golf instruction. It was the exact lessons you'll find in this book!

I said to Lilia, "I'm going to help you become the best Lilia Vu the person. As that journey takes place, your golf will take care of itself." That's exactly what happened. Over the next six and a half months, we worked together: me imparting a blend of my father's and my life lessons, and Lilia putting in the hard work of applying these lessons to her own life and her game. These lessons became strong tools, which she then took into her next season on the Symetra Tour, hoping to win her LPGA card back.

Now remember, the top ten money winners get a card to the LPGA. Guess where she finished on the money list that year? *First.* She won three tournaments, was awarded Symetra Tour Player of the Year, and earned her spot in the LPGA Tour for 2022. In a little over a year, she'd completely turned her life around. Not only did Lilia lead the money list with $162,292 in winnings, but she easily led the tour in smiles and gracious confidence. Her eyes were sparkling again, on and off the golf course. This was not just due to her golf results; it was a combination of regaining her total love of golf and developing her appreciation and gratitude for everything golf had given her: the fun of competition, an excellent education from UCLA, and a multitude of friends. Also, as I reminded her, she was actually getting to pursue her passion for her career!

Inside Lilia was a flower waiting to bloom. It just needed a little help. I don't know what your goals are or what struggles you're facing. But I know there's a flower inside of you too. So I'm going to say the same thing to you that I said to Lilia: if you are open to it, I think I can help you. Instead of thinking your dreams are unattainable and seem almost impossible, give this book a chance. What worked for my father, for me, for Lilia, and for the others I've mentored can work for you. You can be the best!

CHAPTER 1

BECOME THE BEST

ONE OF THE first lessons I learned from my father was to be the best. "I don't care if you're cleaning toilets," my dad would say. "Make sure they shine!"

This wasn't just a figure of speech; he meant it literally. When he was a prisoner of war, one of his duties in the camp was to clean the latrines. He took the task seriously—more seriously than his fellow prisoners of war thought he should. "Ziggy, don't clean them so well, 'cause it's making us look bad," the other soldiers would say. "Come on, Ziggy! They're just toilets."

But that's not what my father was about. He didn't clean well to prove a point. He took pride in a job well done. And frankly, that work ethic likely saved his life. The sad truth is that in the camps, your ability to work had a big impact on whether you survived.

For my father, no matter the job, there was never a reason to do it less than your very best. If you were going to do something, you should do it 100 percent. He would tell me, "Don't ever let anyone say Johnny Ply doesn't work hard and doesn't do a great job, no matter what you're doing." I took that advice to heart, and now, when I mentor people today, I always encourage them to become the best at what they're doing.

YOU HAVE ONE GOAL AND ONLY ONE GOAL

When I first started working with Lilia Vu, she was in the middle of a slump. After a stellar collegiate career at UCLA, she'd made it to the LPGA, only to lose her playing card. So she set the goal in her mind: I'm going to earn my way back onto the LPGA. Seems natural to think this way, right? But that was actually the wrong goal.

While we were at lunch one day off the golf course, I brought up the subject of goals. I looked Lilia in the eye and said, "Lilia, your goal is not to get back to the LPGA."

She looked at me incredulously, like I had three heads. "What are you talking about, John? That's my only goal!"

"No, it's not," I said. "Your actual goal is to become the best player on the LPGA."

She stared at me again. It was a big goal—the kind of goal that can feel overwhelming and impossible. But I wouldn't have said it if I didn't believe she had the skills to achieve it! I've watched and played a lot of golf. I know talent when I see it.

"It's a much longer goal. It's a long path, like this," I explained, spreading my arms wide to show her what I meant. "It's going to be bumpy. There's going to be ups and downs. But you can never lose sight of this goal: to be the best." As long as she kept working towards that goal, riding out all the bumps along the way, I knew she could make it. There was a pause in our conversation, and as Lilia mulled over my words, I could tell she had never before considered this goal. I could see the excitement growing in her eyes. She was beginning to realize what I said was true: she *could* become the best. Setting a big goal for yourself can be deeply motivating.

Sometimes, we pick the wrong goals. The goal we set for ourselves is not the goal we actually need to succeed. We underestimate what we are capable of, and we limit our potential by setting our sights too low. If you instead strive to become the best, you give yourself room to unlock and discover your true potential. For Lilia, if her only goal was to get back onto the LPGA, then that might have been all she achieved. She could have ended up like so many professional golfers who get a card and lose it in just a year. Instead, during her fabulous success on the Symetra Tour, she never got content, because she had a much bigger goal. As she was dominating that tour, in her interviews, she politely answered the typical questions, but ultimately, she would say, "I still have a lot of work to do!" Because her goal is to become the best player on the LPGA, she has not only made it back to the LPGA but has also placed highly in several tournaments. She's already achieved more than her initial goal, and I can't wait to see what she achieves next.

IT'S ABOUT EFFORT, NOT RESULTS

Now here's the thing: there are no guarantees. You may not reach your ultimate goal on that long and bumpy road. That's not the point. The point is to see how far you can go. You don't want to go through life not trying, because one of the worst things you can do is lead a life of regret.

When I arrived at Indiana University, it was the time of the legendary coach Bob Knight. My sophomore year, the Hoosiers men's basketball team went 31–1. The next year, they improved to 32–0 and won the NCAA Championship. That championship team was considered one of the best college basketball teams of all time.

That was also the year I tried out for the team. During my senior year in high school, I led my team as captain, and my very good friend John Crockett and I were considered two of the best shooters in the state of Illinois. Still, the chances of making a storied team like the 1975–76 Hoosiers as a walk-on were next to nothing. But I knew it was something I had to do, or I'd regret it. So when open tryouts were announced, I went.

The first day, there were thirty-seven of us who all wanted to be on the team. First day, eight or ten left. The next day, five more left. Day three, another three or four more get cut. This went on for ten days of grueling tryouts. I managed to make it to the final day, when only eight of us were left. I wasn't tall enough or strong enough, but my pure jump shot had certainly caught the coaches' eyes.

I had Bob Driscoll, my grade school basketball coach, to thank for that. Through sixth to eighth grade at Saint Catherine of Siena, Coach Driscoll spent endless hours drilling me on the fundamentals of a great jump shot. He had me watch videos of Jerry West, Rick Barry, and Rick Mount, three of the best jump shot shooters ever in the NBA. He would have me wear ankle weights and taped weights to my wrists as well. Then he set up a ten-foot ladder on the court, and I had to take shots from behind the ladder, jumping as high as I could and shooting over it. My jump shot was pretty ugly at first, but by eighth grade it was good with a perfect follow-through.

Because of Bob Driscoll's mentorship—and a whole lot of practice—I had a chance to become part of basketball history. For a team this good, they weren't going to take just anyone. But there was a rumor Coach Knight was going to take one of us! One of the final eight happened to be the brother of a star on the team and had heard as much. Suddenly, chances that had started as slim-to-nothing looked a whole lot better.

They called us in. "Thank you all for trying," one of the coaches said. "But unfortunately there's no one among you who can fill a need on this year's team."

They cut us all!

Was it disappointing? Of course. But did I lose something by trying? Not in the least bit. I took a chance of pursuing a passion of mine and gave it my very best, and I even got to see a Bob Knight practice. I continued to play high-level intramural basketball at Indiana, with a highlight of scoring fifty points in one game, along with excelling in many other sports at Indiana. I was actually voted athlete of the year in my senior year, so I did become the best in a way that was deeply rewarding for me.

What I remember most about those tryouts was the feeling of hope. I remember the hope of getting to sit on the bench, wear those cool uniforms, do the warmups, and maybe, when the team's up by thirty or forty or fifty points (as they often were in those days), get a little floor time. I'd get to be a part of the Indiana University basketball team and be a part of history. In striving to be the best, hope is a crucial ingredient. You have to really believe it's possible.

I knew my chances of making the team weren't great, but I remember my nineteen-year-old self saying, "John, you will regret it if you don't at least try out." I don't feel like a failure because I didn't make it onto one of the best basketball teams of all time. That's not how success works. Success is something that is felt internally. You feel successful when you can take pride in what you've done, which means it's your effort, not the result, that matters. Had I never tried at all, that's when I would have felt like a failure. In the end, because I gave it my best effort, I had become the best basketball player I could be. That's what it really means to be the best.

THE GOAL GUIDES THE DECISIONS

Even though there are no guarantees, it's important to strive to become the best because your goal is your compass that will guide all your decisions.

When I started my first company—Priority Food Processing—I knew we couldn't be the biggest in our industry. But we could become the best.

Priority Food Processing was a service company. We blended and packaged powdered food products for other companies. So being the best meant offering the highest level of service in the industry, at the most competitive price for the value we provided. That goal was even right there in the company's name: Priority Food Processing. What did that mean? That name said that we were in the food processing business, and you, as our customer, were our top priority. As the customer, it was your product, your formula and ingredients, and your name on the packaging. It was your reputation you entrusted to us, and so we made it our reputation to be honest, never cut corners, and always do our best. If we made a mistake (which rarely happened), we'd rectify it immediately and compensate our client. This is how I sold our services.

With my guiding goal in mind, all my decisions became clear. I always knew what I needed to do. With every decision, no matter how small, I did the things that would take me closer to providing the highest service and best value to our customers. For example, in order for us to be the best for our customers, we needed the best employees and the best suppliers. The way you get the best employees and suppliers is by treating them well. So that's what I did (more on this in chapter 7), and because of it, my employees and suppliers worked really hard to fulfill all our customers' needs. I can't think of a single time where we lost a client to a competitor. Another way we strove to be the best was by implementing the highest standards of quality control and sanitation. We invested in isolated processing rooms and the best dust collection system, and each product we handled was blended and packed in its own clean room, which was something unique at the time.

That one goal—become the best—guided everything we did, from the people we hired, to the salaries we paid, to the equipment we bought, to the prices we set. The best employees. The best suppliers. The best quality control. The best facility sanitation. The best reputation. The best value. The best service. Over time, each of those small decisions to be the best added up, and that's what made my businesses so successful. Being the best isn't a one-time thing; it's something you choose to do every day, until one day, you look back and realize just how far you've come.

YOU NEVER KNOW WHERE BECOMING THE BEST WILL LEAD

Starting the summer after eighth grade, I caddied at the Oak Park Country Club. At all private golf clubs that have caddie programs, you start as a B caddie, and with experience, you can work your way up to an A caddie and then eventually to an Honor caddie, earning better bag fees and tips. Today, a B caddie might earn sixty dollars a bag, but an Honor caddie can earn eighty dollars a bag, and that's before the tip.

So I set myself a goal, and by now, you already know what it was: I wanted to become the best caddie I could be.

As a beginning caddie, the job is basic. I'd carry a thirty-pound bag of clubs from hole to hole. When my player took a big chunk out of the grass, I'd carefully put the divots back in. I'd smooth out the sand bunkers, including all of the player's footprints.

To become the best, I had to do even more: my job was to help golfers play their best games, by providing knowledge and advice. With experience, I became an expert on the course and quickly worked my way up to Honor caddie. I'd be on the course every day, usually two times a day, whereas the golfers might play only one round a week. Better than almost anyone, I knew the subtle breaks in the greens that determined how a golf ball rolled. Golfers would often ask me, "What's this putt gonna do?" and I could tell them in exact detail.

Put yourself in the shoes of the golfers for a moment. Imagine you just shot your best round ever, thanks to the advice of your caddie. You're probably going to tip that caddie pretty well, right? Absolutely! By becoming one of the best caddies, I received the largest tips!

But that's not the only reward I got. Becoming one of the best caddies led to so much more, far more than I ever could have imagined.

During my junior year, our caddie master, Bill Survilla, approached me about applying for the Chick Evans Scholarship, which is given annually to caddies at various golf clubs around the country. If you win the scholarship, that's four years of college tuition completely covered, along with housing.

Now, this was a very big opportunity for a kid of my background. Neither of my parents went to college. I was the fourth of five children, and none of my older siblings had yet gone to college either. Winning that scholarship would be life changing.

There were four requirements. First, I needed two years of experience as a caddie, which I already had under my belt. Then, I needed a good academic record and to show financial need—check and check. Finally, I needed to demonstrate I was someone of strong moral character. Because of my work ethic, Bill Survilla, the club president, the head golf professional, and several members of the Oak Park Country Club were more than happy to write letters of recommendation for me.

I was invited to the offices of the Western Golf Association

(WGA), which administers the scholarship. There, I had a one-on-one interview with WGA executive Jim Moore, whose job for many years was to screen applicants and determine whether you were a good person or not. After that interview, a month or so later, I found myself in a room with two dozen WGA directors, nervously answering their questions. They held in their hands the power to change my life forever.

I didn't know it then, but if you make it to that room, there is a high likelihood you are assured of winning the scholarship. I know this because I've now been in that room many times, on the opposite side of the table as a WGA director. For more than thirty years now, I've had the honor and privilege of meeting with many of the young men and women who've been so richly deserving of the financial support that the Chick Evans Scholarship provides. We give out around three hundred scholarships a year and must raise over $40 million annually in charitable contributions to provide these scholarships.

Just before Christmas, I received a letter in the mail from the WGA. My parents and I opened the envelope and we read it together. "Congratulations," it said. "You have been selected to receive the Chick Evans Scholarship to Indiana University." As I read and reread those words, my parents broke into tears. It was one of their proudest moments of me, not only because I was going to college, but because I went out and earned this life-changing award. What a Christmas present!

And that's actually not all. After college, I ended up getting my first job because of connections I'd made while caddying, and that job led to me eventually starting my own companies. So in a sense, everything I've accomplished stems from being a caddie. When becoming the best is your goal, you'll be amazed at how far that goal can take you.

IT DOESN'T MATTER WHERE YOU START

The first year after I started Priority Food Processing, I had the good fortune of meeting and hiring a very impressive young man, Alfonso Acevedo. Alfonso reminds me a great deal of my father. He embodies everything this book is about, and his life is an example of what is possible when one strives to become the very best.

Alfonso joined my company as employee #5 when he was just seventeen years old. Like my father when he first arrived in America, Alfonso spoke little English and quickly decided to distinguish himself through hard work. There was no job Alfonso wouldn't do. He started out in the blending room, dumping bags of ingredients into the mixers; pouring everything into fifty-pound bags, one hundred-pound boxes, or two hundred-pound drums; and stacking these heavy containers on pallets. He learned how to wash and sanitize our large blenders between each order. He was always on the lookout for opportunities to acquire new skills. He learned to drive a forklift and operate the packaging machines.

He worked every day to improve his English, through trial and error but also through the classes my company started to provide. Eventually, through persistent hard work, Alfonso rose through the ranks to become our head production manager.

Alfonso and I became good friends, and it's been amazing to watch his personal growth over forty-plus years. We worked together for thirty-five years, and he was with me through many major changes. He was there when I started my second company, Pinnacle Food Products, and when we merged the two companies into what became Insight Beverages Inc. In a way, he was actually with my companies longer than I was, because he stayed for another six to seven years after I retired and sold Insight Beverages to Kerry Foods. We often joke about his starting pay. I'm certain I started him at $3.75 per hour, but he insists it was $3.25. Either way, by the time he retired at age fifty-seven, he was earning six figures annually plus more in bonuses. In fact, he became so indispensable that Kerry Foods, a multinational company, sent him to oversee special projects in Mexico and even had him help out at other Kerry plants.

Alfonso has been enormously successful in his personal life as well. He met his amazing wife, Sheryl, while working with her at Priority Food Processing. They eventually raised wonderful twin boys in the beautiful home they own. They both worked hard, invested wisely, and put their sons through college while also enjoying the occasional material comfort, such as the 900-horsepower modified Mustang that Alfonso got as his personal gift to himself for his amazing work career.

Like my father did, Alfonso always smiles. There's a gentle kindness about him, which is why so many of his coworkers looked up to him and why he is so well liked. He's one of my top five favorite people in the world. During the last third of his business career, Alfonso developed a love for playing golf, and I like to think I had some influence in that. We're still close friends, and we golf together a few times every year at Chicago Golf. I can clearly remember how poorly he played early on, but he approached golf with the same work ethic he used to retire at such an early age. It warmed my heart when he told me he went and competed in his first official golf tournament last year in Mexico. A lot of amateur golfers, even experienced ones, are often afraid to put their golf game into competition. But Alfonso wasn't afraid to fail, because he learned long ago, the only real failure is not trying!

Alfonso's story emphasizes an important lesson: it doesn't matter where you start. You can start as employee #5 at a scrappy food processing startup making $3.25 (or $3.75) an hour, meet the love of your life, work hard, raise wonderful kids, and win the admiration and respect of everyone you work with—essentially, live the American Dream. We're all dealt different cards in life. You might wish you'd been dealt a better hand, but life doesn't come with re-deals. All you can do is play your best with what you have.

Wherever you are in your journey right now, whatever cards you've been dealt, you can become the best.

BE THE BEST "YOU"

Being the best is a lesson my father carried with him his whole life. When I was building my growing companies, I remember buying a used packaging machine, and we hired my retired dad to clean it. This thing was absolutely filthy, covered all over in caked-on food powders that my father had to chisel away with a scraper. It was a task most people wouldn't want to even touch. By the time my dad was done with that machine, it looked brand new. He always took pride in jobs like that, but I think this one was especially meaningful to him because he got to be a part of the business I was building. His efforts saved us a great deal of money too. A brand-new machine would have been $250,000, but we were able to buy and refurbish the used machine for $50,000.

In truth, my father was always a part of the business, long before this, because he played such a big role in helping me become the best version of myself. That's what being the best is really about. It's about becoming the best "you" that you can be, not any one individual goal. People are so focused on achieving external goals—be it the next promotion or the next award—that they forget to focus on the internal. They don't ask, "How can I be a better person?" But it's just like I told Lilia: "I'm going to help you become the best Lilia Vu the person. As that journey takes place, your golf will take care of itself."

Everything starts with becoming the best version of yourself. When you continually focus on becoming a better version of yourself, the exterior parts of your life have a way of improving. Be the best "you," and everything else tends to take care of itself.

CHAPTER 2

PURSUE YOUR PASSION

MY FATHER, ZIGGY, the most successful person I've ever known, was a man who followed his heart. He believed you should follow your passion within—even when outside forces push back against you. For my father, his biggest passion in life was my mother, a woman he dearly loved.

Growing up, my parents would drag my brothers, sisters, and me to church every Sunday. It's what good Catholic parents did for their kids. We'd sit on the hard pews listening to the service and struggle to stay awake. Then, when it came time to receive Communion, my parents would send us up to the priest while they remained behind. It was a mystery to me why they never took the Eucharist.

Several years later, my sister Mimi passed on a story that Ziggy had told her about deciding to marry our mother, and I finally put two and two together.

My father met my mother at the butcher shop where he worked a second job every afternoon. According to him, it was love at first sight. My mother was a regular customer, and her visits were the highlight of his day. Soon, they agreed to meet outside the shop. My mother invited my father to a picnic to meet her parents and her best friend Lila. When he arrived, he saw my mother playing with a baby. Initially, he assumed the boy belonged to her friend, but the baby was actually my mother's (my older brother Dave). She'd been married previously and had been waiting for the right moment to tell him.

When my dad found out that the baby was my mom's, he knew in his heart that he needed to be that baby's father. There was a problem, though. My father was a devout Catholic, and the Catholic Church did not recognize divorce. So according to his religion, he could not marry my mother. Remember also that this was the early 1950s, when divorce was both less common and more looked down upon, even before bringing religion into it.

By then, however, my father had fallen deeply in love. He looked within himself. What his inner faith told him was this: he should marry the woman who'd captured his heart, and he should also become a father to her young son. That night, after the picnic, he prayed. The next morning, he woke to a beautiful rainbow. When he saw that rainbow, he thought, *I have my answer.* He believed God was telling him, "Yes, it's okay, Ziggy. Do the right thing, marry that woman, and raise that child."

This story might sound unbelievable to you, but to me, it's a beautiful lesson about how the heart will never lead you astray. It's also a lesson about how inner faith can and will prevail when external "rules" tell you that you can't do something.

In the first twenty-five years of their marriage, my parents went to Mass but could never take Communion. Over time, views on divorce changed, and my parents sought and were given absolution. For the rest of their lives, when it came time to receive Communion, they didn't watch from the pews. They joined the other parishioners.

I'm not a big church-goer myself, though my dad certainly was. However, I do have a strong belief in faith. For me, faith means following your heart—pursuing your passion and doing what you think is right, as my father did. Practicing my faith has led me to finding purpose in life and doing meaningful work for others.

In the introduction, I talked about what success is and isn't. It's not about money or accolades. Success is a life well lived. You will often be told what you should do by external forces—by the media, your church, coworkers, your friends, or even your family. But success is defined internally. Only you can decide what it means for you. That's why it's so important to pursue your passion.

FROM DOCTOR TO NAVY SEAL:
A LIFE OF PASSION LEADS TO SUCCESS

Let me tell you a story about Jeff. I've known Jeff since he was five years old. He was best buddies with Zach, my eldest son. As kids, their favorite game was cops and robbers. Our neighbor had given my son a real police officer's shirt that came down to his ankles. He would be dressed to the nines—holster, hat, handcuffs, real police shirt—and rarely could we get Zach to take the outfit off, which meant poor Jeff was often stuck playing the bad guy.

Around the age of eight or nine, my son discovered the Navy SEALs, and he decided that's what he wanted to be when he got older. Jeff liked the idea too. They talked about the Navy SEALs constantly. Joining an elite team of fighters must have excited their young imaginations. Eventually, Zach found other interests, but becoming a Navy SEAL never really left Jeff's mind.

Fast-forward just over a decade. Jeff was now a junior in college. He was taking pre-med courses in preparation for a medical career. His father was a doctor, his mother was a nurse, and his older sister was already in medical school. The medical field was sort of the family business, and Jeff's parents would have been thrilled for him to follow in their footsteps. Jeff, however, was not very excited about this future.

One day, I got a call from Jeff out of the clear blue sky. "Mr.

Ply," he said, "I'd love to meet up with you for lunch. I'd love to talk about my career plan."

"Sure, no problem," I told him. We met for lunch, and I asked him, "What's on your mind?"

Jeff said, "When I used to come over to your house, I remember you saying, 'If you can pursue your passion for your career, that's the ultimate.' Do you remember saying that?"

I did remember saying that. And I was surprised to hear my words repeated back to me. I told my kids this all the time: pursue your passion. My career had to do with blending and packaging food powders (think hot cocoa mixes, taco seasoning, etc.). As you can probably imagine, I wasn't particularly passionate about that. It was just something I found after leaving college because I needed a job.

Because I lived the other side of things, I've always believed that pursuing your passion is the ultimate career path, if you can do it. Because when you're passionate about your career, it's no longer something you do just to make a living. It's something you do because you must do it—your heart is telling you that you need to do it. Doing something you love won't ever seem like work because of the great passion that lives within you. When your passion becomes your career, that's the greatest career of all, whether you're a singer who loves to sing, a painter who loves to paint, a basketball coach who loves helping players perform at their absolute best, a doctor who loves to heal, or a teacher who loves to help young minds grow.

So I made sure my kids heard this from me and heard it often: Do what's in your heart. Pursue your passion.

Well, apparently Jeff heard this message too, during one of the many times he was over at our house, and he remembered it. He told me, "Well, Mr. Ply, my passion is to become a Navy SEAL, but my parents don't want me to go down that path. And that's why I wanted to come talk to you."

So I hit him with many questions. First, how serious was he? You have to be very fit physically and mentally to even contemplate a career as a Navy SEAL, and even then, fewer than 10 percent of candidates make it through all the training. I asked Jeff why he thought this was something he wanted to do.

Jeff straightened in his chair and looked me directly in the eye. When they were boys, he said, my son Zach had planted the seed in his mind. The seed might have died and never sprouted, if not for a second key moment while attending Christmas Mass with his family. Among the parishioners was a Marine home from duty, sharp and serious in his dress blues. Seeing that Marine, Jeff felt inspired. The seed that had been lying quietly dormant at the back of his mind began to germinate. He wanted to serve his country too. He also was drawn to the idea of being a part of an elite team, where every person wanted to be there, just as much as the next.

"Mr. Ply, it's been on my mind my entire life," Jeff said. "It's something deep inside me that I just want. I believe it's my true passion and calling!"

Now, the last thing I wanted to do was come between parents and their child. At this moment in time, Jeff was on the path to becoming a doctor. He was a great student and doing well in his coursework. But his heart was telling him something different.

"Jeff, here's the deal," I said. "Your parents are going to hate me for the advice I'm about to give you. But I think you should pursue it, because I think you'll never forgive yourself if you don't. Your passion to become a Navy SEAL is so strong. Your belief in yourself is so strong. Though the odds are against you, I believe you have the will to do it!"

Jeff took my advice and followed his heart. There was a passion that lived within him, and it had been burning ever since he was a kid.

Heart was exactly what he needed to succeed—to push through the months and months of the toughest and most vigorous physical, mental, and emotional challenges that constitute Navy SEAL training. During Hell Week, he and the other few remaining trainees had to spend several hours in the ocean off the coast of San Diego, helping each other out and keeping each other afloat. Jeff was pushed to his physical limits. The day before, he had eaten something that didn't agree with him, and he hadn't been able to eat or drink much after that. He became so dehydrated that the instructors temporarily pulled him out of training to give him medical aid. They filled him with four bags of IVs and four Ensure drinks and threw him back into training.

In a typical intake, about 250 individuals will begin training to become a Navy SEAL. Of these, roughly two dozen will make it. Jeff graduated and spent the next ten years as a Navy SEAL. He was deployed five times and became a troop commander, with roughly forty SEALs under his command. When he hit the ten-year service mark, he left the SEALs for civilian life, and now he applies his leadership skills and work ethic in the business world.

Jeff is the ultimate success story to me, because he made his passion his career. He looked within himself and found the path he was meant to follow. I promise, it can be the same for you. Your heart won't ever lead you astray. Pursuing your passion is a fundamental step towards achieving your own definition of success.

WHAT DOES IT MEAN TO LIVE A LIFE OF PASSION?

I am a great believer in pursuing your passion as your career, but it's important not to allow your career to take over your identity as a person. Take, for example, my mentee Lilia Vu. If you recall, when I first started working with Lilia, I said to her, "I'm going to help you become the best Lilia Vu the person." Emphasis on person.

Throughout her life, Lilia had unknowingly identified herself as "Lilia Vu the golfer." Golf was who she was, and to the casual observer, if you see someone who lives, eats, and breathes golf, this can look very similar to passion. However, we made it our goal to help Lilia become the best "Lilia Vu the person," not the best "Lilia Vu the golfer."

Why is that distinction important?

Being a golfer is a crushing way to identify yourself. Think about it. Tiger Woods, the greatest player in the world, had the highest winning percentage of any golfer in the last century. He won about 25 percent of his tournaments, which means he lost 75 percent of the time. He lost more than he won! If you identify yourself by how well you play golf, you're going to have a miserable life, because that's just the nature of the game. In golf, you're going to have many bad days that far outnumber the good ones.

For Lilia, she found golf as a young girl, competed all the way through high school, competed at UCLA for four years, then went out onto the LPGA to fail for the first time in her life. She went into a spiral. It can be spiritually and emotionally crushing to fail at something that you've made central to your life.

This is why I wanted to guide her back into being the best version of Lilia Vu the person she could be. I knew if she did, the golf would fix itself.

I'm going to let you in on a secret about passion. We don't have one singular passion in life. We have passions, plural. If you identify yourself based on your career, even if that career is a passion for you, you're limiting yourself. You're not giving yourself room to pursue all your passions and live your most successful life.

It's also important to recognize that passion can come in many forms. For my father, Ziggy, his greatest passion was loving my mom. He would say to her, "Honey, you bring me heaven on earth." For me, growing up, basketball was my passion. Then golf became my passion. Pursuing your passion doesn't have to mean making it your career. It just means making it a part of your life in some way.

Here's another secret about passion. It can be found in unexpected places, and sometimes it's not found at all, but created. As I mentioned, I certainly wasn't someone who dreamed of blending and packaging powders since childhood. Yet in the running of my two businesses, I discovered there were things I was passionate about, such as helping and motivating people. As a sales guy, I was passionate about winning customers and helping to solve their problems. This, in fact, was a key factor that brought us so many customers. When a potential client sees a young, enthusiastic person who's passionate about helping them, they want to do business with him.

In essence, what I discovered is a business is made up of people, and I've always been passionate about helping people. If you can find ways to create passion in your work, you will find what you need to be successful.

WHAT HAPPENS WHEN YOU LOSE YOUR PASSION?

Sometimes people lose their passion, and that's a sad thing to watch. For whatever reason, the thing that brought them so much joy is making them miserable. If a person has lost their passion, it's most likely because somewhere along the way, they've forgotten how to have fun.

There's a young man I started mentoring recently. His name is Luke, and he's a very intense and driven person. He's also a great golfer, and like Lilia Vu in her early career, he identified himself closely with the game.

Luke's story is interesting precisely because of his drive and intensity. In his freshman year of high school, he lost the state high school championship to another freshman, named Tommy, by eighteen shots!

Tommy sort of became a rival, and every time Luke stepped out onto the green to practice, he would use the memory of his stinging loss as a motivator. He became laser focused on his game, almost to the exclusion of everything else. Luke would just tell himself, "I am going to win the state high school golf championship."

The intensity of focus paid off. In his junior year, Luke defeated Tommy (who, by the way, later became his best friend in college) and won the state championship. In his senior year, he ranked as the top high school golfer in the state. Both feats were accomplished through sheer drive and determination.

Luke then went to college on a golf scholarship, but his play took a complete 180. Suddenly, what worked previously—sheer drive and determination—wasn't enough anymore. But these were the only tools Luke had developed. His coach wasn't much help either. So Luke fell back on what he knew: more focus, more drive, greater determination. It was a formula for heartbreak. After four unsatisfying years of college play, Luke left lacking confidence, and sadly he had lost some of his love for golf.

By the time I met Luke, it had been a very long time since he'd allowed himself to have fun or enjoy the game of golf. The very first time I played with Luke I noticed he hit every shot at 100 percent effort and launched the ball sky-high. So I came up with a plan to help him fix that part of his game. Luke had no idea what was in store for him.

A few days later, we met at Chicago Golf Club for a breakfast meeting and discussion before we planned to play eighteen holes. Luke's younger brother Nick, another fine golfer, was practicing at the driving range when we arrived. I asked Nick if he wanted to join us, and he replied, "Sure!"

When we got out to the first tee, I took Luke's driver out of his hand and said, "I will pick each club for you throughout the round." Luke's typical first-tee confidence and excitement quickly turned to a look of uncertainty. Nick, on the other hand, had a huge smile on his face, almost holding back a chuckle.

Now, each golfer hits fairly consistent distances with different clubs. In choosing Luke's clubs for him, I was doing two things: (1) making him end up in places on the course that he wasn't used to and (2) forcing him to adjust his swing.

To start, instead of using his driver, I had him tee off with a 3 iron, which hits about 80 yards shorter than his driver. That left him 170 yards from the green, farther away than he was used to being. No problem—he could simply use his 9 iron, with which he typically hits 170 yards. Except instead of his 9 iron, I gave him his 7 iron, with which he normally hits 190 yards. This meant if he didn't adjust his swing, he'd overshoot the green. This exercise continued for the remaining seventeen holes. If he had a 130-yard shot, he was required to use his 150-yard club.

For the first twelve holes, Luke was not enjoying this task, as he was hitting shots from places he would have never found himself in had he been using his preferred clubs. His ball flight and distance were difficult to control, and he struggled to hit the correct yardage. He even chunked a couple of iron shots, which means hitting the ground well before the ball, which is embarrassing to a player of his skill level.

We changed his putting too, which looked rigid and mechanical. At breakfast, Luke had told me how much he loved to play basketball, so I said, "Here's what we're going to do. No practice strokes. Today you're going to putt like you're shooting a basketball. In basketball, you don't have time to think. You react. You look and you shoot." Almost immediately, he lost his stiff, mechanical motion. There was a softness in his putting stroke, and he putted beautifully throughout the round after adopting a completely new putting routine.

After the thirteenth hole, Luke really began to embrace this exercise. On the fourteenth hole, he had loosened up, and his swing had gotten much slower. On his approach shot (the shot meant to land on the green), he landed the ball just six feet from the flag—while using a club that was two clubs more than his normal. He then sunk the six-foot putt for a birdie with no practice stroke!

I said, "Are you having fun now, Luke?"

He looked up from his best hole of the day and smiled. "Yeah," he said. "That was pretty cool."

Luke rattled off three consecutive birdies, and smiles and fun started to replace the early frustration.

Losing some of your passion can be heartbreaking, when the thing that once filled your heart brings you unhappiness versus enjoyment. When that happens, there's only one thing you can do: start having fun again. In Luke's case, the key to getting that fun back was getting him outside his comfort zone and changing things up a little. If you've lost your passion, take the pressure off yourself. Stop worrying about the external results and just have fun.

WHERE DOES YOUR DRIVE COME FROM?

Passion and drive are closely connected. If you lose your passion, you'll lose your drive, and if you're driven by the wrong things, you'll end up killing your passion. To keep the passion in your heart, you have to be driven by the right things.

First of all, you can't be driven by money only, because even if you're making a lot of money, you're never going to be completely fulfilled. Someday you'll wake up one morning not as excited to go to work. The average work day is eight hours, or nearly one-third of your waking life. Do you want to do something that pays well but doesn't really fulfill you for eight hours a day? Or do you want to do something that makes you excited to get up each and every morning?

Competition for competition's sake is not a great driver either. Consider Luke. A competitive mindset helped him achieve results for a while, but eventually, it became the very thing that made him feel frustrated and unhappy. If you measure success by beating someone else, then as soon as you're not winning, you'll begin feeling like a failure. And remember, nobody, not even Tiger Woods, wins all of the time!

For the longest time, I was motivated by the fear of failure, and that wasn't healthy. I was fearful of letting my parents down and later, after getting married, I was fearful of letting my family down. It had been that way ever since I was a kid. I would think to myself, John Ply cannot give up. John Ply cannot fail. John Ply cannot let anyone down. By twenty-three, I became the president of the company I was working at. At age twenty-five, I had started my first company. Most people would look at me and say I was successful, but I was still so afraid of failure that I was not able to enjoy my early success.

Being driven by fear is entirely different from, say, an Olympic athlete who is driven by the dream of success. They have a dream of standing on the podium and feeling the gold medal being placed around their neck. They visualize that success and that feeling. So they stay in the pool longer if they're a swimmer, they practice harder if they're a gymnast. They practice, practice, practice, all the while keeping that dream close to their heart. If they lose a contest along the way, they shake it off. Their failures mean nothing to them. Only the wins matter. They say to themselves, "I'm not stopping," until their gold medal dream is reached.

Compare that with being motivated by the fear of failure. The fear of failure is felt in your stomach. It's heavy and burdensome. Whereas the thrill of winning is felt in your heart. It's joyful and electric.

It's okay to be a driven person. You can't get anywhere without a high degree of personal motivation. But be sure to examine whether your drive is coming from the right place. Ultimately, your drive needs to come from the same place as your passion. It needs to come from your heart.

YOU KNOW BEST

Pursuing your passion isn't always easy, but it's always worth it. My father Ziggy loved my mother very dearly, and he put that love before all else.

My mother fell ill in her early sixties. She was in significant pain for about five or six years and spent her last year bedridden. She'd always been a big-hearted woman, but her illness and pain made her very hard on people around her, including her loving husband. We tried to get outside help, but she wouldn't have it. She chased them all away. Only my dad was allowed to take care of her. He did everything—all the shopping, cooking, cleaning, and caring for her. He took care of her every need, and he never complained. He felt he was doing his duty, and as far as he was concerned, the sun rose and set on my mother.

My father could have chosen not to marry my mother and take on the responsibility of becoming a father to her child. He could have chosen to not take care of her at the end of her life. Arguably, those would have been the easy things to do. But loving her was his passion, and he did it until the day she died. Even after she passed, for the next fourteen years, he fixed his bed every morning and laid out framed photos of her across the pillows— his Lorraine Ply shrine. Hardly a day went by when he didn't mention her memory. It wasn't always easy, but loving her gave him "heaven on earth."

As a man guided by his heart, my father would often tell me, when I was faced with difficult decisions, "Trust your gut. You know best, Johnny. You know best." I think that's true for all of us. When my father's heart and faith conflicted, he knew best what to do. When you, too, are struggling, all you have to do is listen to your heart. You know best the right path for you.

CHAPTER 3

USE ALL YOUR TOOLS

FOR MOST OF my dad's life, his job was simple: cut meat. Of course, "simple" does not mean easy, unskilled, or unimportant. For thirty-five straight years, cutting meat was my father's livelihood—the thing that allowed him to raise five kids and build a home. And he was good at it. Every Thanksgiving, he'd carve the turkey, and when he was done, it was nothing but a skeleton. He would carve off every last ounce. He was an artist with his knives, just like Van Gogh with a paintbrush.

After my father died, I didn't want any money or any valuable possessions in terms of dollars. First of all, he didn't have anything of significant financial value. Even if he did, I didn't need it. But I did want *something* of his—a memento to remember him by. I mentioned this to my youngest sister, Shirley, and her husband went through their closet and pulled out an old fedora my dad used to wear. I was glad to have it because my dad always wore a hat when he went out, and it provided a warm reminder of him.

But in truth, his hat was not what I wanted. All I really wanted was my father's knives.

As you can imagine, a butcher's knives are some of his most prized possessions. My dad had a personal set of four knives and two knife sharpeners. Every time after using them, he would carefully clean them, dry them, wrap them in newspaper, then a towel, before packing them in the trunk of his car. Those knives went everywhere with him.

After he died, we lost track of the knives for a while, but then my sister Mimi told me she thought our brother Rich might have them. I called up Rich, told him how much I really would like the knives, and two days later, he had them delivered to my house in California.

Once I had them, I realized I didn't really know what to do with them. They were sharp and almost ominous looking! I definitely wasn't going to carry them around in my trunk like my dad. If I ever got pulled over, the police would probably think I was a serial killer and arrest me. These knives were *big*, and though they had to be sixty years old, they were still very sharp.

Eventually, my very creative wife, Cynthia, took the knives and had them mounted in a glass case with a small wood plaque inscribed with "Ziggy's Knives."

When Cynthia gave me this gift for my birthday a couple of years ago, it immediately brought tears to my eyes. It was such a special gift for me, because those knives are more than just knives.

They're a representation of who my father was. There's also a lesson hidden in those knives: to be successful, you need many quality tools.

There are some who believe an artist is only as good as their tools, while others believe blaming the tools is merely an excuse. I'm inclined to believe the truth is somewhere in the middle. Talent and skill will take you far. But if you don't develop a deep understanding of all the tools at your disposal, you will never live up to your full potential for success.

THE RIGHT CLUB MAKES ALL THE DIFFERENCE

Now, my father was a butcher, but I'm not. So instead of trying to explain different kinds of knives and no doubt *butchering* it, I'm going to talk about something I understand well: golf.

In my time as an amateur golfer, I have gotten a hole in one on par 3's ten times. That's pretty good, considering most golfers never get even one. (US Hole in One estimates the odds of an amateur golfer getting a hole in one on a par 3 hole at roughly 12,500 to 1.) So I'm doing something right here. But what I'm actually just as proud of is the number of times I've knocked it straight into the hole from the fairway, from 100 to 225 yards out, which is basically equivalent to a hole-in-one: almost a hundred times over my fifty-five years of playing golf. This isn't because I'm a golfing prodigy (I'm definitely not). My secret is simply this: I always

YOU CAN BE THE BEST

try to use the right club, and of course then I hope my shot flies towards the flag on the green.

A golfer typically has fourteen clubs in their bag. This includes:

- The driver, which is typically used to begin most holes and to hit the farthest distances
- Irons, which come in different sizes used for more specific distance ranges (for example, depending on your technique and strength, a 9 iron might go 130 yards for you, an 8 iron will go 140, a 7 iron 150, and so on)
- Wedges, which hit the ball up higher and are typically used for shorter shots and also to get yourself out of tricky spots such as "deep rough" (very tall grass) and sand traps
- The putter, which is used for, you guessed it…putting, which is rolling the ball into the hole

Every club is built for a different hitting distance and situation, so a lot of becoming a great golfer is learning which clubs to use and when. When you choose the wrong club, the ball isn't going to go where you want it to. But when you choose the right club, based on your personal hitting ranges and course conditions, you can put the golf ball within yards of where you want it to go.

It's the same in life. You can read all the books on success that you want. Each book will give you different tools for your toolbox. But you need to know *when* to use those tools.

So how do you do that? Practice. In order to learn which club to use, I've taken the time to meticulously measure exactly how far I hit the ball with each club. And I've done this in multiple conditions, because guess what: the right club depends on the circumstances. When it rains, a golf course goes soft and almost squishy. Now, when the ball hits the ground, instead of bouncing and rolling, it almost sticks to the ground and stops immediately. In contrast, very firm ground, or a strong wind blowing behind you, can cause your shot to go ten, twenty, or thirty yards farther than normal.

Throughout this book, as I explain the lessons, I'll be sharing stories about how my father lived these lessons and how I and people I've mentored have used them too. These stories will give you an idea of when and how to use the lessons, but ultimately, you need to use all the tools at your disposal. You have to figure out how to make these lessons work for you. And you have to learn how to use them in different situations—not only when it's easy and the lessons come naturally, but also during the challenging times, when it's tempting to do things the easy way instead of the right way. Just like every golfer has a different selection of clubs for what works best for them, every person has different ways of using these lessons that will work for them. No two paths are the same, but we can learn a lot from each other—which is the whole point of this book!

THE CLUBS OF SUCCESS

I'd like you to think of all the lessons in this book as your personal knives, clubs, or tools—whatever metaphor works for you. But I also want to introduce you to what I call the "clubs of success."

You might not be a golfer, but bear with me for a moment, because golf makes for a pretty good metaphor for life. In golf, you have a goal—the hole—and you steadily work your way towards it, one swing at a time. Sometimes you hit shots that sail straight to the fairway or the green. Sometimes you mis-hit shots and get off course. Or you get a bad bounce that lands you in the sand trap, and you have to extricate yourself with an excellent wedge shot. Then, after all that work, you finally get the ball in the hole, and guess what: you have to start all over again with another hole. Likewise, life is a never-ending cycle of goals, hard work, obstacles, recovery, and achievement.

Golf is a rewarding sport, but it can be frustrating too, because just when you think you've mastered it, you'll have a series of bad shots that knock you down a peg and keep your ego in check. I can't count the number of times I've heard diehard golfers declare, "I hate this game!" That's how life is too. We love life but hate much of what happens to us in life. We hate the mistakes and the obstacles and the goals that always feel just out of reach. But just like in golf, in life we have to learn how to deal with what we're given and make the best of it.

Here's another way golf and life are similar: on every single golf course and with every single life goal, no matter how different, your fundamental strategy remains essentially the same. In golf, you start with the driver, get closer with irons, overcome obstacles with wedges, and bring it home with the putter, ending with you making the shot and sinking the ball into the hole. In life, you start with commitment, get closer with strategy, overcome obstacles with recovery, and bring it home with consistency, ending with the completion of your goal: achievement. These are your clubs of success.

Driver: Commitment

In chapter 1, we discussed why "becoming the best" should be your one and only goal. It's the biggest, most inspiring goal you can set for yourself. When you decide you want to become the best, step one is commitment. You have to commit to get anywhere. Otherwise, as soon as things get difficult (and things always get difficult when you chase big success), you'll give up and abandon your goal. Commitment is your launching point, just as the driver is in golf. It's your way of saying, *I want _____, and I'm going to put in the work to get it.*

In golf, the driver goes the farthest, but it also tends to go the most wild. It gives you the least amount of control over the ball, which can be scary. Commitment can be scary too, which is why some people struggle with it. You can't be sure your commitment will pay off. Maybe you dive into something and end up failing or getting so far off track that you're even farther from your goal than before. It's possible. As long as you're committed, you can work your way back to where you want to go. But if you *don't* commit, you'll definitely never make it. So take the chance on yourself and commit to becoming your best!

Commitment means different things to different people, but it always means putting something on the line. That could be time, energy, money, or something else. At twenty-five, I quit my job and started my first company, Priority Food Processing, using a $15,000 loan from my parents (which was almost all the money they had), a $30,000 investment from my business partner/client, and a $15,000 bank loan at an extraordinarily high interest rate of 23 percent. At the time the prime rate had reached 21 percent, and my loan was at 2 percent above prime. Honestly, it was a horrible time to start my own company, but that ultimately was a good thing because it pushed me into survival mode. I was committed out of sheer necessity. My wife and I had just bought our first home and only had savings for about two mortgage payments. Failure wasn't an option, so my focus was always on doing everything to succeed. I began with a single goal: *We can never be the biggest, but we can be the best!* With that goal in mind, I grew Priority Food Processing slowly but steadily, starting with just one employee. My drive and our goal to be the best never diminished, even when my survival was no longer on the line.

Commitment is vital to getting the ball rolling (or, ideally, *flying*) in your endeavors. It's appropriate that commitment is the metaphorical driver, because commitment is what drives you to work towards your goals. But commitment and drive are not the only things you need. In golf, even if you commit and pull off a perfect drive, that doesn't guarantee success. It's great to get off to a good start, but you still have to overcome other obstacles afterwards. If you don't strategize properly or stay motivated, you can lose your momentum and risk not reaching your goals or dream.

Irons: Strategy

Once you've used your driver to launch the ball, your game should get increasingly purposeful. You want to be strategic in your swing, which clubs you use, and where you aim the ball to get the best score. Irons are designed for this, which is why they represent strategy in the game of life. These clubs are the strategic things you have to do along the way on your journey to achieve your goals.

Strategy largely comes down to making correct decisions. Should I do this? Or should I do that? Should I buy another blender for my business? Should I sign up for that class? Should I apply for that job out of state? Making the right decisions, just like choosing the right club, comes down to experience. It involves a lot of trial and error. You have to make decisions and then pay attention to the results to figure out whether you got it right or wrong. Then you take what you learned to hopefully make better decisions in the future.

Your life-irons are also the strategies you use that contribute to your progress—things that help you to make the right decisions. In golf, you have seven different irons, but for life, I've simplified it down to just three.

#1: Measure Your Results

Remember: becoming the best is a long goal, and with long goals, it's easy to lose focus or get off track along the way. You cannot set a goal and rely on hope alone to achieve it. To get results, you need to *measure* them. Measuring your results gives you a way to assess what you've achieved, where you're currently at, and what you still need to do. Only by measuring your results can you figure out what's working and what isn't, and adjust accordingly.

When I was running my two businesses, we measured *everything* to ensure that each day we were making progress towards our goal of becoming the best.

For example, as a part of providing the best customer service, we strove for better on-time-delivery numbers. Our clients expected their product to be delivered by a certain date, and we tracked delivery times and whether we were keeping our promises to clients. We also wanted to run the cleanest plant anywhere in the industry, so we hired an outside company to perform regular inspections and give us a grade. We measured and graded ourselves on safety too. When you're running a manufacturing business, you can't have people getting hurt. Safe working conditions were paramount. We also tracked areas where we could become more efficient, for example, by reducing ingredient and product obsolescence. We measured exactly how much raw material we lost to things such as waste, damage, and spoilage.

You'll notice that all the things we measured related to our goal of becoming the best. "Measuring" isn't the point. Measuring *what matters* is the point. You need to very clearly define your true goal and then search for metrics that measure your progress towards that goal. For example, maybe your goal is to get into the best shape of your life. Depending on how you define "the best shape of your life," you could track any number of metrics: body weight, running distance or speed, weightlifting reps, sugar intake, and so on.

When you aim to become the best, you need to define for yourself what becoming the best means, and then you need to measure it.

#2: Incentivize Performance

The other challenge with long goals is a loss of motivation. Incentives can keep you focused and working towards your goal.

At my companies, once I knew what metrics to track to gauge our performance, I used bonuses, benefits, and other rewards to incentivize employees to perform their best. If our on-time deliveries improved, that triggered a reward. If the sanitation inspector gave us a better grade, that triggered a reward. Incentives were a powerful tool to focus attention on areas for improvement and keep everyone on course to becoming the best company.

Incentives work on an individual level too, which is why I used them while mentoring Lilia. I mentioned in the introduction that Lilia's golf game didn't need much work. The one thing I felt she needed to improve on was her irons accuracy and distance control. I figured because of how the 2020 Symetra Tour had gone for Lilia, particularly with the cancellations due to COVID-19, she could use a little financial boost. So I told her, every time we golf, she was going to have an opportunity to earn some cash. Make a birdie? You earn a $100 bill. Make an eagle? You earn $250. Hole it from the fairway? You earn five $100 bills. Make a hole in one? That's ten $100 bills. There were consequences for bad holes as well: any hole that she scored bogey or worse, it cost her $100 (though of course I would never make her pay me her own money; she could only lose what she'd earned from me).

This approach gave Lilia a financial incentive, sure, but more importantly, it made her slow down and think about each hole individually. I wanted to change her level of focus and awareness throughout her overall game and begin to focus on the power and possibility in front of her with each swing.

Needless to say, by the time Lilia left for the tour in March 2021, my wallet was lighter, and she had a cigar box full of cash.

You can apply incentives like this to yourself. They can be positive (rewards for desired behavior or results) or negative (punishments for undesirable behavior or results) or a combination of both. The most important thing is they must be *motivating*. Essentially, incentives are a way to encourage yourself and others to make the best decisions. Since we're all motivated by different things, you may have to experiment to figure out what works best for you.

#3: Assess and Adjust

Once you reach a milestone, it's important not to become complacent. You can't be happy with the status quo. Becoming the best is not a one-time thing. It's a continual process.

No matter what you achieve, there's always room for improvement. Success isn't standing in place. At my two companies, we were never satisfied with our metrics. If we hit a target one year, it wasn't our goal to hit the exact same target the following year. We raised the bar. We continually challenged ourselves, striving each year for higher benchmarks (and higher bonuses too!). I told our employees that if we did everything in our power to become better as a company, we would never have to worry about the competition, because our competition would never catch us.

Whatever the timeframe—be it a day, a month, a year, or longer—assess what you've accomplished and adjust as needed. Look at where you've been and where you're going, and then ask yourself two questions: "Do I need to do anything differently?" and "What can I do to get even better?"

Wedges: Recovery

Each decision you make impacts your chances for success in the near and distant future. So the better you get at making decisions, the greater your chances for success. But nobody hits the ball perfectly every single time, and you're not always going to make the right decision. Sometimes you're going to make mistakes or poor decisions, or you will encounter bad luck, and that's where your wedges come in.

When one of your trial-and-error decisions turns out to be the latter, you have to figure out how to get back on track, right? In golf, when you get into a bad spot—like a sand trap or deep grass—wedges are how you get out of it. This is called *recovery*. In life, too, when things aren't going the way you hoped, you need to find solutions, and not give up!

In both golf and life, you have to adapt as situations—good and bad—arise. In our analogy, wedges represent the adaptability and problem-solving you use to recover from missteps and falls on your path to success. It's the only way to make it back onto your personal journey to being the best.

Some obstacles are predictable and have a specific tool helpful for the situation. Like how in golf, if you end up in a sand trap, there's a good chance you'll be using a sand wedge to get out. You can prepare for these obstacles ahead of time and improve your recovery through research—reading books and articles, talking to those who have been through similar situations, and so on.

Other times, the obstacles you face aren't predictable. They come at you out of nowhere. The key is to not panic. Panic never helped anyone's game. You can't prepare for every possible scenario, but you can prepare to face everything as it comes and approach the problem as level-headed as possible.

Once, we were blending a product for one of our service customers, and one day we received a call from them accusing us of causing a salmonella contamination in their product. This could have potentially put us out of business.

Had we panicked, we might have shut down our whole plant. That would have meant delays in production as well as phone calls to all of our customers to explain the situation, which could have potentially damaged our reputation and our client relationships.

Fortunately, we didn't panic. We had faith in our rigorous quality control procedures and high sanitation standards. We had retained samples of every lot of product we produced, and we sent them to a lab to test for salmonella, along with swabs of our equipment. All the tests came back negative, proving the salmonella didn't come from our plant. As it turned out, my customer's client that bought the product had salmonella contamination in their own plant.

On the path to your goal, things might get difficult, but that doesn't mean all is lost. On the golf course, if you get into trouble, you can still get a par or even a birdie . . . as long as you hit a good or great recovery shot. It's the same in life. Challenges *will* arise, but as long as you are willing to work through them, you can still achieve your goals.

Putter: Consistency

Though its hitting distance is far shorter, the putter is just as important to a successful game as the driver. It's often the putts made near the hole that make or break your score. Once again this is true of both golf and life.

The putter represents the habits, routines, and other small details you attend to on your path. These are integral to progressing on your path to success, and you must practice them to develop consistency. No golf professional ever wins a tournament without making a lot of putts.

The first thing I do for everyone I mentor is give them a copy of *The Slight Edge* by Jeff Olson. It's a great motivational book that talks about the power of small, daily choices. As Olson says, "What you do matters. What you do *today* matters. What you do *every day* matters. Successful people are those who understand that the little choices they make *matter*, and because of that they choose to do things that seem to make no difference at all in the act of doing them, and they do them over and over and over until the compound effect kicks in."

Every day, life is about making choices. Everything we do, each day, is a choice. Recognizing that automatically gives you a slight edge in life. If your goal is to lose weight, every meal is a choice. Is eating the double cheeseburger and fries going to bring you closer to your goal? Or is eating the salad? Those are choices you make. It might seem like one is "easier" than the other, but really it's quite simple. Which do you want more? To achieve your ultimate goal or to enjoy that one meal that is taking you farther away from your goal?

All day, every day, choices are in front of us. These tiny decisions are what ultimately separate successful people from everyone else. People who consistently make the "right" choices (the choices that lead towards their goal) experience success, and people who routinely make the "wrong" choices (choices that lead away from the goal) fail. Whatever success means to you, it won't happen overnight, and whatever your goals are, you won't achieve them with a snap of your fingers. You have to keep choosing the things that serve your ultimate goal, again and again. If you start to recognize and leverage the power of your choices, you can sink putt after putt.

SHARPEN YOUR KNIVES

My youngest son, Andrew, was at my house not long ago, and when he saw Ziggy's knives, he immediately called dibs on them. He pointed and said, "I want those." (Meaning after I die!)

Ziggy's knives are a fitting legacy of him, because they're a symbolic representation of so much more. In those knives, you can see his decades of hard work, his perseverance, and his care and gratitude for the tools that allowed him to provide for his family. Even more than the knives, Ziggy's true legacy is his lessons about life—the lessons you find in this book.

In golf, no one club is more important than the others. You need them all. The same applies to the lessons of this book and the clubs of success: commitment, strategy, recovery, and consistency. To get where you want to go, you need to use all of them. A lot. Repeatedly. The more comfortable you get with the clubs of success, the faster and better you'll get at achieving your goals.

One of the remarkable things about my dad's knives is you can see how much they were used. Each time you sharpen a knife, you shave away a bit of the metal. My dad sharpened those knives so many times that each blade is probably half the size it once was.

That's how I want you to approach the clubs of life and all the lessons of this book. Use them again and again, and when you feel the lessons dulling in your mind, come back and read this book again to sharpen them. Keep sharpening your knives, and success will come.

CHAPTER 4

NEVER GIVE UP, NO MATTER WHAT

IN THE MORE than five and a half years my father, Ziggy, spent in a POW camp, he witnessed unspeakable atrocities and saw firsthand the evidence of gruesome crimes committed during the Holocaust. Many days, he didn't know when he'd eat again, or if he'd even live to see the end of the day.

Take a moment and think about what that experience would feel like. The constant anxiety. Fear. Uncertainty. Hopelessness.

It was an environment designed to break people—their bodies and their spirits. But my father knew that if he was going to survive, he couldn't give up, no matter what.

So he made himself useful. He did what his captors told him. He worked around the camp. He cleaned those latrines I told you about.

I told you in the previous chapter that his work ethic likely saved his life. This is more than conjecture. Because he was a good worker, he was assigned duties at a nearby farm. One day, when he came back to the camp after working at the farm, several POWs had mysteriously disappeared. No one ever saw those men again. Had my father not been away, it could easily have been him.

My father was nearly twenty-five years old when the war—and his time as a POW—ended. He couldn't go back to Poland due to Communist rule, so he spent nearly five years working for the US Army. He lost the prime years of his life, from the age of seventeen when he joined the Polish army to the age of twenty-nine when he received his discharge papers from the US military. Those years are a time when many of us today are going off to college and starting our careers. I started my first business at twenty-five, an age when my father was just leaving the POW camp to work for the Allies.

After the war, my dad rarely talked about his time as a prisoner. He couldn't without crying. The things he experienced there caused deep wounds, the kind that never really heal. I think the only way he was able to deal with it was to push it down really deep, so that's what he did.

Even when faced with unimaginable, soul-scarring horrors, he never gave up. It's an example we can all learn from. We will all face obstacles and challenges of some kind—it's what we do when they arise that will determine our success.

PERSISTENCE PAYS OFF

While my experiences can in no way compare to my father's hardships, I learned my own lessons about not giving up around the same age he did, in my early twenties.

After leaving Indiana University in 1977, I went back to Chicago with my finance degree hoping to land a job at a bank. I interviewed with several banks, but no one would offer me a job. Later, I learned from someone in the industry that no banks were hiring undergraduates that year. They were only interested in hiring those with MBA degrees.

Here I am, with no job, about to get married. What do I do?

A mentor of mine, John O'Neill Sr., came up with this idea. He said, "John, I think you should write letters with a resume and send them to all the country club members you used to caddie for."

I was willing to try just about anything then, so I said, "Okay, I'll do that." I had caddied at the Oak Park Country Club for seven years. Off the top of my head, I could easily think of fifty members I used to caddie for that I could send the letters to.

John said I should handwrite the letters, as it would be more personal and leave a greater impression. This meant each one had to be perfect. I couldn't misspell a single word, or I'd have to start all over. I couldn't smudge the ink, or I'd have to start all over. I spent three days writing letters and finally completed the task. Do you know how easy it is to misspell a word, even though you know the spelling?

I sent out fifty letters and waited a few days, then followed up with phone calls. I went down my list alphabetically. I was nearly midway through the list when I got to George Lauritzen, a gruff old guy I'd caddied for at Oak Park. He owned a food blending and packaging business, Lauritzen and Company, in Wheeling, Illinois.

"I might have something for you," he said over the phone. "Why don't you come up and see what we have to offer?"

George Lauritzen and I walked around his plant, which seemed like a vibrant place. About 130 people worked there. Hundreds of different powdered food ingredients and packaging materials came off the trucks. They were blended and packed, then truckloads of finished goods went out the door each day.

Lauritzen said he needed someone to do inventory control. Truthfully I didn't really know what the heck that was. But something else he said caught my attention. "This is a great company. If you work here, you'll learn everything there is to know about running a business."

The pay was low—$10,000 a year, about half of what my fellow college graduates were making—but I liked the idea of learning how to run a business. Also, Lauritzen said pay raises were tied to performance, and that appealed to me as well. It's how I've been motivated in my life: work hard, do the best possible, and the rest will take care of itself. This worked for me in basketball and caddying. I figured it would work for me in business too.

This all took place about a week before my wedding. Mr. Lauritzen and I shook hands, and he hired me on the spot.

I'd found my first job thanks to caddying and a very tedious but ingenious idea from a mentor!

NOTHING TO LOSE,
EVERYTHING TO GAIN

At that point, my not giving up wasn't that impressive. I didn't have any choice to do otherwise. Either I found a job, or I wouldn't be able to help support my wife and myself. But I was about to be really tested.

Our biggest client at Lauritzen and Company was Pillsbury. They made up 95 percent of our business. They owned everything: the ingredients, the formula, the packaging materials. We were a manufacturing business that provided the blending and packaging service to our clients.

Everyone was happy because capacity was filled. No one had an inkling to ask, *Hey, is this a good idea to have all our eggs in one basket?*

I was ten months into the job when we all learned the answer to that question. My direct boss, a thirty-two-year-old guy, misquoted a huge project. Pillsbury was rolling out a new product nationwide, and our company was supplying the blending and packaging service. We're talking hundreds of thousands of cases.

He quoted and signed the contract for thirty-five cents a case, when in reality, we needed more than a dollar to cover our costs. In other words, we were losing our shirts to the tune of seventy-five cents a case.

To make matters worse, the product wasn't selling. Pillsbury had product in warehouses, product on grocery shelves, and none of it was moving. And here we are, Lauritzen and Company, bringing more bad news, saying, "You know what, guys? You owe us way more money. We misquoted the job and can't do it for thirty-five cents! And not only can we not do it, you need to pay us what we've lost for the cases we already produced." It was easily a quarter of a million dollars.

Well, it got ugly. U-G-L-Y.

I observed everything, like a fly on the wall, George Lauritzen and his accountant going back and forth with the folks from Pillsbury. Name-calling from both sides and no productive negotiations occurring! In the back of my mind, as I was listening to these heated exchanges, I was thinking, *Isn't it better to lose this battle and later win the war?*

In this case, George pushed and pushed, and he eventually won the battle. Pillsbury wrote a giant check to make our company whole financially. Within a week, though, Lauritzen and Company lost the war. Pillsbury sent a convoy of trucks to take everything they owned out of our plant. Out walked 95 percent of our business!

It doesn't take a genius to know what happened next. Layoffs. My direct boss, naturally, was fired because he misquoted the project and so he had to go. But the biggest casualty in all this was the plant workers. More than one hundred lost their jobs! The place emptied like a ghost town. As the new guy, I thought I'd be next. I wasn't there even a year, I was newly married, and I was about to lose my job.

Well, shockingly, that didn't happen. A few days after the layoffs, George Lauritzen came to my office. "John," he said, "I'm gonna teach you how to sell, and we're going to save this company."

What do I know about selling? I thought. *I never sold anything in my life!* Then again, I didn't know anything about inventory control when I started either.

Realistically, Lauritzen and Company was a sinking ship. I could have easily bailed. But I thought to myself, *What do I have to lose?* I was still young, not even twenty-three years old, and George promised me $60,000 a year plus part ownership of the business if I could help him turn the company around. Back in 1978, $60,000 was beyond my wildest dreams. So from my perspective, I had nothing to lose and everything to gain.

When you're faced with challenges and you're thinking about giving up, ask yourself, "What do I have to lose?" If you think about that question, the answer is usually nothing. And don't forget to ask that all-important second question: "What do I have to gain?" If you give up halfway, you'll never find out.

THROWN INTO THE DEEP END, SINK OR SWIM

Here is how George Lauritzen taught me to sell. He didn't! He set up five sales calls on the East Coast—Nabisco, RJ Reynolds, Nestlé, and two smaller companies—and he bought me a plane ticket. He threw me into the deep end. Sink or learn to swim. I didn't go with anybody, and I didn't yet know the exact capabilities of our business. I was just twenty-three years old. Never flown in a plane or rented a car. And there I was in New York and New Jersey with sales calls set up with a couple of the biggest names in the food industry.

I will never forget my first meeting, because it lasted barely ten minutes. The buyer would ask a question, and I wouldn't know the answer. I tried to project as much confidence as one could in that situation. "Sorry," I said. "I don't know, but I'll find out for you."

The buyer would ask, "What's your annual blending capacity? How many cases can your packaging line produce? Can you do a two-stage fill, a three-stage fill?"

Each time, my reply was the same. "Sorry, I don't know, but I'll find out for you."

It was a disaster.

The rest of the trip went just as badly. My appointment at Nestlé headquarters in White Plains, New York, was set for ten thirty in the morning. I drove over there and arrived a half hour early and sat in the massive lobby. When ten thirty arrived, the buyer didn't come down. The secretary in the lobby said, "Sorry, Mr. Ply, can you please wait another thirty minutes?"

Sure, no problem. I had come all the way from Chicago. But another thirty minutes went by, and another thirty minutes. The lady came over again, very apologetic, and said it would be a bit longer.

Finally, after a couple of hours of waiting and thumbing through magazines, she came back a third time and said, "Mr. Ply, I'm so sorry. He won't be able to see you today. Catch him the next time you come to White Plains."

I learned so much about sales on that first trip. Key among the lessons is when you're selling, you're going to be disappointed. People are going to cancel. There's a lot of rejection, and there's nothing you can do but try again. Never give up.

Anything new you take on is going to be challenging. That's what learning and pushing ourselves is all about. If you choose to let something that is hard push you down, and you stay down, then you're making a choice in that moment. If you choose to get back up every single time you get pushed down, you're making the choice to believe in yourself and your ability to learn and grow and improve. Few things come easily to any of us, and those that do come easy tend to not seem as valuable. When you push through hardship and sacrifice and adversity, you value yourself and the outcome that much more.

My first sales trip had been a disaster, but I'd gotten something valuable out of it. I'd learned that I needed to know everything about our company. (A three-stage fill, by the way, is when you can put three different items into a single pouch.) I went back to Chicago and knuckled down. I walked around the plant learning everything there was to know about our capacities and capabilities, so next time I'd be prepared.

I went back out there and knocked on doors. I remember going to San Francisco and landing Hills Bros. Coffee. Not only was it new business, it was something new for us. Hills was a messy but high-paying job to package freeze-dried coffee in a stand-up pouch. That was exciting, and it felt particularly rewarding because I had to work so hard for it. When you're faced with challenges, it's important to take time to celebrate the small wins like this and feel proud of your accomplishments. That pride will help keep you motivated.

Within two years, I had brought in fifty different food companies and successfully diversified the company. We no longer relied on a single customer. More importantly, we had turned things around.

WHEN QUITTING ISN'T GIVING UP

George Lauritzen promoted me several times during my initial years with him. From inventory control to production control, to assistant vice president, vice president, and then president of Lauritzen and Company. After my first year, he raised my pay from $10,000 a year to $20,000. However, during those two years I helped rebuild the company, my pay never rose above $25,000, even after I was appointed president.

My promised $60,000 salary kept getting put off because we weren't fully stabilized yet, which I fully understood. But we got to the point where we were doing almost $2.5 million per year in service work, and still my pay never budged. I had killed it for more than two years, helped save the company, and my compensation didn't reflect the effort.

Finally, as my wife and I were nearing the purchase of our first house, I got George to increase my salary to $32,400. He did give me papers to sign that gave me an ownership piece of the company, which helped me stay motivated. Unfortunately, a couple of weeks later, he said he couldn't commit to the ownership piece, and he made me sign new documents taking the ownership option away!

Our working relationship began to fray. Even more than the dispute over pay and the broken promises, it was the constant nitpicking that wore me down. I did all the selling, the scheduling, and the motivating of our employees. I developed all the new contacts/customers. My office became the centerpiece of activity at the company, and George resented that. I think it was probably jealousy, because *he* used to be the one in charge for many years. Still, he was in his late sixties, and he could have been golfing at Oak Park Country Club, letting the twenty-five-year-old he trained run his business and make money for him.

But instead, he'd sit in my office, looking over my shoulder. Every time the phone would ring, he'd say, "Who's that? What was that about?" He'd fall asleep sitting in a chair in my office. Can you imagine your boss in your office all day long?

Our relationship was becoming more complicated. George didn't have many friends and was estranged from his two sons. So I was employee, friend, and stand-in son all wrapped in one. We ate lunch together, golfed together. I'd spend twelve hours a day at the office with him. Then at night, I would go home and receive at minimum four calls from him wanting to talk about this or that.

Towards the end of my career at Lauritzen and Company, George began to look for ways to undermine me and micromanage. For instance, I was still in charge of scheduling production. He'd go out in the plant and demand, "Why isn't that line running?"

"Well, John hasn't scheduled it," the workers would explain.

"Goddammit, I own this place. Start that line up!"

The workers would do it, because what else could they do? And then the entire schedule was thrown off.

Things finally came to a head following a small mistake out on the production floor. I had no control over what had happened, but George tried to blame me for it and embarrassed me in front of a couple of employees. I got so mad, I picked up my briefcase and said to him, "When you get your act together, give me a call."

Now, no one ever quits on George Lauritzen. He fires you. It took him about a minute to realize what was happening. By then I was already out the door, backing up in my car, when I saw in my rearview mirror George come running out after me. I didn't stop. I just left. And in my heart, I knew I was never setting foot in his company again!

This chapter is about never giving up, and here I am telling you about quitting a job. Well, there's a saying, people don't quit jobs, they quit bad bosses. In my case, I was quitting George Lauritzen. With the constant nitpicking and undermining from George Lauritzen, I got to a place where I felt stuck, and that's a bad place to be. You never want to feel as though you can't leave—because you have a great title or your pay is too good—and then you don't have the guts to quit and try something new.

This is why I've never thought of my decision to leave Lauritzen and Company as giving up. I've always thought of it as taking action to turn a bad situation into a better situation.

Remember me saying I had nothing to lose and everything to gain? Well, I never ended up gaining what I was promised. And arguably, I "lost" a few years of my life to that company. I felt a genuine sense of loss. All the work I had put into turning the business around—it felt like it was for nothing. But you know what? I've never regretted my time at Lauritzen and Company.

When you choose to pursue something, it means investing time, energy, or even money. But even if your pursuit doesn't end up working out, what you invested isn't "lost." It's the payment for hard-won lessons. In my case, I may not have gotten what I initially wanted (my $60,000 salary and ownership in the business), but I got something better: business know-how.

When George hired me, he said I would learn everything about running a business. He was right about that, because that's exactly what I did next. Within two months of leaving Lauritzen and Company, I had set up my first business: Priority Food Processing. I had also hired my first employee and landed an investor who was our first client.

I had quit a difficult boss and an untenable situation. But I never gave up, and I never quit on myself.

LEAVE YOUR BAD MOMENTS BEHIND

Life isn't all flowers and sunny days! There are dark days, but that's the beauty of life. To fully appreciate life's successes, you must experience the setbacks along the way and work through them. It's overcoming obstacles that gives life great satisfaction. Think about what life would be like if everything was perfect all the time. It would eventually become dull and monotonous.

Overcoming obstacles is what makes you stronger. Remember me telling you how Lilia Vu finished first on the 2021 Symetra Tour? Well, getting there wasn't so simple. She had a slow start to the season, and there were many bumps along the way.

Take, for example, her third tournament of the 2021 season. It was in Arizona at the Casino Del Sol Golf Classic. Lilia played strongly throughout the weekend and found herself leading the tournament with eleven holes to go, possibly about to get her first professional win. Then she had a potentially confidence-depleting stretch of holes. Bogey. Triple bogey. Bogey. Bogey. In just four holes, she fell dramatically down the leaderboard, from first to twenty-fifth.

A lesser golfer might have lowered their head and given up. But not Lilia. She shook off those bad holes and never gave up! She played the last seven holes in four under par to tie for third. Then, two weeks later, Lilia won her first tournament of the 2021 Symetra Tour in Kansas.

Sometimes, things can be going so well for you, and then, in the next moment, you find yourself in a deep hole and think, *I'll never climb out of this. I will never get back to where I was.* Yet the key to winning is putting bad moments behind you and continuing to move forward. Another book I recommend to everyone I mentor is *The Golf Mystic*, by Gary Battersby. It is a book that is just as much about how to live life as it is about golf. It says, "The ball is always in your court when it comes to choosing how you're going to react to anything. You can either dwell on it... or you can choose otherwise and move on." Disappointments and challenges will happen, and often you can't control them. But you can control how you respond to them. Instead of getting discouraged and dwelling on the negative, focus on the next opportunity, then the next opportunity, and then the next.

The ability to leave bad moments behind is what makes Lilia a true champion. She never allows a loss or bad hole to eat away at her. She just focuses on what comes next. She keeps going and never gives up. I started calling her "the Bounceback Queen of the Symetra Tour"!

I was reminded of this watching her compete in the 2022 US Women's Open, which is one of the five major LPGA championships. Lilia had just come off some of the best weeks on tour, finishing in third place the week before, which at the time of this writing was her highest finish for the year. She started the Open feeling confident but maybe a little exhausted from playing seven matches and finishing third the previous week.

On the first day, she shot par. On the second day, two under par. On the third day, par again. Going into the final day, she was in seventeenth place. But then Lilia birdied three of the first eight holes and jumped to fifth place. Suddenly, she was five under par for the tournament, and her many fans and I were getting excited because it looked as though a giant payday was coming her way. After eight fantastic holes starting the final day, Lilia was looking at a fourth- or fifth-place finish.

Guess what happened on the last ten holes? Triple bogey. Double bogey. Par. Par. Double Bogey. Par. Triple Bogey. Bogey.

Par. Par. She went from five under for the tournament to six over and finished in thirty-fifth place.

Now this is what I love about Lilia. I messaged her to make sure everything was okay. I thought she might have been exhausted or, even worse, injured. She messaged back: "Hi John. It was just a series of bad lies and being humbled by a US Open course. I won't let a couple of bad holes diminish these last two great weeks."

I love that attitude! That perspective! This is how I know Lilia Vu is a true champion and will most likely reach her ultimate goal of becoming the best player on the LPGA. Most people would be in tears after a day like that. Not Lilia. She held her head high and didn't let a bad day diminish her recent success. That's what it means to never give up. Lilia took the next two weeks off and bounced back with a top-ten finish in her third major of the year, the KPMG Women's PGA Championship.

ATTITUDE IS EVERYTHING!

To me, the most remarkable thing about my father isn't just that he never gave up, but that he kept a positive attitude through everything. Henry Ford is famous for saying: "Whether you think you can, or you think you can't—you're right." My father was someone who always thought, *I can*. I remember he once came home early from work, which never happened. It turned out he had been laid off that day from Swift and Company after twenty years! He was the sole provider for our family, so losing his job must have been demoralizing. But looking at him, you wouldn't know it. That's what he was like. He didn't waste time on negativity or disappointment. Within a week, he found a new job at New City Meat Packing, where he worked for the next fifteen years until he retired.

In the end, never giving up is all about attitude. Keeping a great attitude and thinking positively is crucial for a winning mindset and success. I talk about the importance of attitude so much, and try so hard to keep a positive attitude no matter what, that my friend Gary Battersby recently emailed me a quote from Charles Swindoll, saying he thought it was my "daily mantra":

The longer I live, the more I realize the impact
of attitude on life. Attitude, to me, is more important than
facts. It is more important than the past, than education,
than money, than circumstances, than failures, than
successes, than what other people think or say or do.
It is more important than appearance, giftedness, or skill.
It will make or break a company...a church...a home.
The remarkable thing is we have a choice every day
regarding the attitude we will embrace for that day.
We cannot change our past...we cannot change the fact

NEVER GIVE UP, NO MATTER WHAT

that people will act in a certain way. We cannot change
the inevitable. The only thing we can do is play on the
one string we have, and that is our attitude...
I am convinced that life is 10% what happens to me
and 90% how I react to it. And so it is with you...
we are in charge of our Attitudes.

I marvel every time I read those words. It articulates so well how
I've sought to approach my life. If you can go through life with
a positive and enthusiastic attitude—whatever it is you're doing
or whoever you're with—it's infectious. People love to be around
people who are positive, enthusiastic, friendly, and happy. Positive
things tend to happen to people who think positively. And that
all leads towards the ultimate definition of success.

So stay positive, and never give up, no matter what!

CHAPTER 5

<hr/>

FIND A WAY

THE CAMPAIGN TO free Europe began on June 6, 1944, with the Allied invasion at Normandy, and by spring the following year, American troops had liberated the camp in Germany where my father was held prisoner.

With his renewed freedom, my father set to work right away making himself useful to the US Army. In April 1945, Private First Class Zygmunt Plywaczewski and other men in his unit took up positions as guards. They kept watch over German prisoners, ran patrols, and did police work as well.

The Americans made my father the leader of his unit. In a cita-
tion letter, an officer described him as "honest, faithful, and capable of being in charge of the Polish Guard." That sounds exactly

like the man I know. In another letter, a captain said my father and other Polish soldiers were "hardworking and trustworthy individuals" who had "never given cause for reprimand or court martial" nor "shirked their duties in any way."

My father continued to improve himself and assumed positions of authority and trust. In 1947, he completed civilian guard training at the Non-Commissioned Officer's School and earned a "Very Good" rating. The following year, he was made supply sergeant for his unit, responsible for the equipment his men needed to carry out their duties. He also received a vocational certification from the International Refugee Organization, which qualified him to perform farming work.

Zygmunt Plywaczewski worked for the US Army for fifty-eight months as the Allies rebuilt Europe. When he was finished, the Army gave him three choices: he could go back to Poland, he could get on a boat destined for Australia, or he could make a new life in America.

Well, there was nothing for my father to go back to in Poland, which had fallen under Communist rule, and the boat to Australia was full, so my father chose a passage to America. His discharge papers, drawn up on March 1, 1950, described him as efficient and of "excellent" character and recommended him for immigration to the US without prejudice.

His boat, the *General Greely*, departed from Bremerhaven, Germany, on March 15. My father had in his possession: a blue garrison cap; a field jacket; work gloves; a blue shirt and matching trousers and overcoat; a necktie made of cotton mohair; one pair of shoes; two pairs of underwear, three pairs of socks, and two undershirts (all made of wool); two woolen blankets; a face towel; and a duffel bag in which to carry everything. It was all he had in the world, along with his final paycheck from the US Army, which amounted to $40.

The boat he boarded was unbelievably cramped, dirty, and cold. My father crowded into tight quarters with the other passengers, many of whom were traveling by sea for the first time. As the ship crossed the Atlantic, it encountered storms and rocked violently, and the vessel became overwhelmed with vomit and the stench of sickness. My father thought the boat would sink, or they'd all succumb to illness. All he could do was pray. After what seemed like endless days of seesawing and sickness, Zygmunt Plywaczewski finally arrived at Ellis Island on March 27, 1950.

He had no plan, no support network, and almost no money. He didn't even speak English. He'd picked up a word or two from the American soldiers, and he knew a smattering of German from his time in the camp. He could only really speak Polish—a huge hurdle for a man arriving on American shores for the first time.

It was not an insurmountable hurdle, though, because what my father lacked in language abilities he made up for with courage. He was the type of person who always found a way.

After arriving in New York City, my father took any job he could find. He did janitorial jobs and low-level work others didn't want to do. Eventually, he saved enough money to buy a train ticket to Chicago, where he'd heard there was a large Polish community. Chicago was where he found employment as a meat cutter and butcher, and it was where he met my mother and started his family. During these early years in America, his bosses and friends began to call him Ziggy. Then, in 1956, the year after I was born, my father followed the advice of friends and legally shortened the family name from Plywaczewski to Ply, which sounded more American and was easier to pronounce and of course spell! From then on, the Plywaczewskis were known as the Ply's.

America has been called "the land of opportunity," but the thing about opportunity is that it comes down to choices. My father ended up having an incredible life in America because he built that life. It takes grit to leave everything you've ever known to begin life anew in a foreign land. My father always believed in moving forward. No obstacle could set him back for very long.

His ability to find a way, no matter the obstacle, is something I've always admired. Emulating that quality in him has been important to my own success. The things you want in life will not always come easily, but with courage and honest hard work, you can find a way.

THE CADDIE THAT COULD

My brothers and sisters and I grew up poor, so we became early entrepreneurs. Actually, first we became realists. Pocket money was something we needed to earn—no one would hand it to us. We delivered newspapers throughout our neighborhood and cut grass for several of our neighbors. We collected pop bottles for recycling. We even used a bicycle basket to drag the pond for golf balls at Columbus Park Golf Course, our local municipal nine-hole course. We would then sell the balls at a large discount to the golfers playing that day. Our only risk was avoiding the maintenance staff, because they viewed lost balls in the pond as their own! Every time we saw them coming in their yellow trucks, we'd scatter. I remember once we had collected a huge haul of golf balls when we heard them in the distance. We took off running into the woods. The bag was so heavy, we had to ditch it or else we'd be caught. We went back later, but the bag was gone; the maintenance men had found our stash, and we lost a whole day's profits. Still, it was a great little enterprise, and also very fun!

We did anything to make a few dollars. And save a few dollars too. In the seventh grade, I started playing golf with my childhood friend Jeff Thomas, and sometimes we couldn't come up with fifty cents to pay the greens fee at Columbus Park. So we'd sneak onto the tee at the second hole and play eight holes. We wanted to play golf, and we found a way.

Not that I'm suggesting you take shortcuts! There are no short-cuts to success. But in life and in business there are obstacles. No matter how large or seemingly immovable, you have to find a way around these obstacles. My parents couldn't provide my siblings and me with material possessions, but they gave us something far more valuable: the belief that there's no obstacle that can't be overcome. I was fortunate enough to learn this lesson at a young age, and it's been foundational to my success ever since.

I already told you that I used to caddie, but I didn't tell you how—or why—I got started. Caddying was originally just a means to an end. Through eighth grade I attended a Catholic grade school. I wanted to go to the Catholic high school as well. Fenwick High School, it was called, a college prep school in Oak Park right outside Chicago. Fenwick was better academically compared with the public school (where my brother Rich got into fights and almost got expelled). More importantly to me at the time, all my friends were going to Fenwick.

But it was a private school and just too expensive. As much as my parents wanted to send me, they couldn't afford the tuition. So they made me a deal: they would foot the bill for the first semester of my freshman year, but I would have to find a way to pay the rest.

How on earth was I going to do that?

My best friend Jack, who I've known since we were in first grade and who so kindly wrote the foreword for this book, said, "John, why don't you come caddie with me and you can make good money." So that's why, the summer following eighth grade, I went to work as a caddie.

As you already know, it turned out to be among the best decisions of my life, but it was by no means easy. The Oak Park Country Club was five miles from my home, and my only way to get there was by bicycle. I was also a scrawny kid who could barely lift a thirty-pound golf bag. On my first "loop" (the term for caddying eighteen holes), we arrived on the fifth hole, and I was so tired I asked another caddie, "Are we almost done?!" Hardly. We obviously had fourteen more holes to go!

But this was my way—my ticket to Fenwick.

As I grew into the job, I continued to look for ways to become a better caddie and improve my pay. In the early 1970s, caddies earned four to six dollars a bag before tip. However, the stronger and more experienced caddies could shoulder two bags of clubs, which meant two times the money. By caddying six days a week that summer, I earned enough to pay my second semester of tuition. The next summer, I was promoted to honor caddie and was strong enough to start carrying two bags and earn double the wage.

I often carried doubles for thirty-six holes a day and made more than enough to pay for my high school education. I found a way. I created the opportunity for myself, and in doing so, new opportunities opened up to me. Thanks to the Chick Evans caddie scholarship I told you about, I got the opportunity to go to college.

At Indiana University, I made fast friends with the other Evans Scholars, who shared a similar "can do, must do" philosophy. We all lived in the Evans Scholars Chapter House on fraternity row. We didn't have to worry about paying tuition or rent, but our meals weren't covered. So once again, I had to find a way. I went to work in the kitchens of neighboring fraternities and sororities, washing their dishes and their pots and pans. In return, I got to eat whatever they were eating that day. And boy did we eat well!

No matter your goals, there's always going to be some kind of obstacle blocking your path. Success never comes easy, nor should it. The important thing is to always find a way.

THE ENTREPRENEUR THAT DID

In my final days at Lauritzen and Company, I learned a valuable lesson from George Lauritzen, something I'm certain my boss never realized he was teaching me. Fancy titles don't mean a thing. You can rise through the ranks—from inventory control to president overseeing the day-to-day operations of the company—but that impressive-sounding title doesn't mean a thing if you're not given the latitude to run the business free from interference.

Only one title matters in the business world: owner. The owner calls the shots.

After leaving Lauritzen and Company, I decided to become an owner of my own company, Priority Food Processing. The timing was terrible. It was the day before Thanksgiving, 1980, when I decided to leave Lauritzen. It also happened to be a time of stagflation and sky-high interest rates. It was some of the worst economic conditions (outside of the Great Depression) on record, with the US undergoing not one but two economic recessions in a few short years. A month after I quit, the Federal Reserve hiked the prime rate to a staggering 21 percent—a half point shy of the all-time high. I couldn't borrow money because all the banks I went to had the same message: "John, we can't give you a loan while we have hundreds of clients going out of business due to the highest interest rates in history!" But I didn't allow any of that to deter me. If I was going to start my new business, I would need to find a way.

Thankfully, my parents believed in me. They put in $15,000 as a loan, which is all the savings they had at the time. I was friendly with the people at the bank where Lauritzen and Company kept its payroll account, and convinced them to lend me $15,000, at 2 points above prime, or 23 percent. So I was able to raise my $30,000, and I had a potential client lined up who agreed to provide an additional loan of $30,000 in exchange for 49 percent of the business and a sweetheart price for blending his product. With this, Priority Food Processing was born. We launched on January 8, 1981, and blended our first product on January 29—just a little over two months after I left Lauritzen and Company.

I had also hired my first employee—José Arellano, who helped me blend that very first order. Even though I was the owner—really, *because* I was the owner—I was out there on the floor with José, doing the hard work. We filled fifty-pound bags, one hundred-pound boxes, and two hundred-pound drums. We got the powder mixed, the bags filled and sewn shut, and everything stacked at forty bags to a pallet. The work was physically demanding and intense, but also rewarding.

We managed to reach $182,000 in gross service revenue that year. To help survive the year, I had planned on paying myself only a $12,000 annual salary. Unfortunately, even with my wife's income, I *had* to pay myself $18,000 to cover our mortgage payment and other living expenses. Still, that was nearly a 50 percent drop compared with my last year at Lauritzen and Company, when I made $32,000. This is why I tell people, if you're going to start a business, be prepared to make personal sacrifices. After paying employee salaries and accounting for operational expenses, the company netted $5,000 in profit our first year.

But in the subsequent years the business began to grow. Within three years, after reaching annual sales growth of $750,000, I was able to pay off the client's loan—$42,000 altogether ($30,000 in principal and $12,000 in interest). I paid back my parents their $15,000 with interest as well. Remembering my lesson with George Lauritzen, I also exercised my option to buy my client's 49 percent stake so I could own 100 percent of the business. I did this as soon as I could, because the longer I waited, the more valuable the company would be, and the more expensive it would cost to buy out his shares. I bought his stake in the company for $125,000 by securing a new loan. In total, the client netted a great return of $137,000 from a $30,000 three-year investment loan. Win-win! My fundamental belief in doing business!

Let's jump forward by a decade, to another make-or-break moment for the company. It was a time when the future of Priority Food Processing seemed uncertain, and when I'd decided the only way forward would be to do the unthinkable: I would start a second business to become a customer of my first company. My goal would be to replace several of the 120 clients I had worked hard to win over the previous twelve years.

We had grown Priority Food Processing from one little space that we originally rented. As we added clients, we added more space. It got to the point where we had five separate locations—all of them leased—and product was shuttling very inefficiently between each one. One building was almost a mile away from the others.

To maintain our commitment to providing the best service, in 1991, our tenth year of business, I decided to build a beautiful state-of-the-art blending and packaging facility. We installed an amazing dust collection system. We set up individual, isolated, and air-conditioned blending rooms and packaging rooms to keep the powder contained and prevent cross-contamination. We designed and built to our specifications totally enclosed truck docks to keep birds and rodents out for enhanced sanitation. Truly spotless. None of our competitors had anything like it. Most importantly, it brought all blending and packaging under one roof. This was going to be our savior, or so I thought.

Two years into this new facility, we were full. We had so much business our new building was bulging at the seams. We had no place to put anything, and we couldn't keep up with the orders, which meant we couldn't provide the level of service our clients had grown accustomed to. We had too much business and too many clients—which was proof that we were truly the best in our industry. I went to our customers and asked for price increases, but they weren't willing to pay higher service fees. They would threaten to leave and take their business to a competitor, which I didn't realize until later was an idle threat.

We were in trouble. What do I do?

It dawned on me: the machines, the employees, our state-of-the-art facility—they were all working for our clients, but what if they instead worked for us? What if *we* became the client? The plant wouldn't know the difference; it would operate the same way whether we owned the product or not.

This is when I got the crazy idea to start a second company, Pinnacle Food Products. My idea was this new company would become a customer of Priority Food Processing, and it would be able to pay the higher price per pound for blending and the higher price per unit for packaging that I thought we deserved. If all went according to plan, Pinnacle Food Products could possibly become one of our largest customers.

When I floated this idea by one of my closest friends, John Crockett, he thought I was a lunatic! John has sold packaging materials and equipment his entire business career. He works every day taking care of his clients and trying to land new accounts. His mantra is sell, sell, sell, and he is one of the best at what he does. But here I was talking about potentially eliminating most of my customers.

I needed financing to launch Pinnacle Food Products, and the bank was similarly skeptical, but I explained to Fred, my banker, "If I pull this off, you're going to have two great customers instead of one!" Shortly thereafter he got me approved for a $250,000 loan.

Growing Pinnacle Food Products into a successful business was not easy. I hired a product developer on an annual salary of $75,000, and we did a grand total of $0.00 for sales the first year. There were many sleepless nights that first year and the next. Our breakthrough came when I learned about a company called Houston Foods that sold Christmas gift baskets. They needed two individual packets of gourmet hot chocolate to put into these baskets. We developed two Christmas-themed flavors for them: chocolate raspberry in a shiny metallic red package, and Irish cream in a shiny green package. The entire order represented $60,000 in sales, which wasn't great, but it certainly was a nice start to that second year. The pivot away from hot cocoa and into gourmet hot chocolate turned out to be a godsend. As we added several more gourmet hot cocoa clients over the next year, we were perfectly positioned to jump into the new, fast-growing category of flavored cappuccino drinks. Over the next several years, we grew Pinnacle Food Products into one of the largest cappuccino and hot chocolate suppliers in the country. If you have ever purchased French vanilla cappuccino or chocolate supreme hot chocolate in any of the major convenience store chains in the US, you've almost certainly drank some that was produced by our company.

Not only did we survive, we thrived! We solved our space and efficiency problems. We eventually eliminated all of our 120 service clients. And we made a great deal of money—more than $3 per case on our products, compared with the just $0.15 per case we previously made supplying blending and packaging services! Before, my clients were the ones making all the money. Now we were the ones making the money. This new venture eventually brought me tremendous wealth.

Midway through Priority Food Processing and Pinnacle Food Products' tremendous growth, the two merged as one company, and we became just Pinnacle Food Products. Then a few years later, we ultimately changed our name to Insight Beverages. In addition to cappuccino and hot chocolate, we made frozen granitas, lemonades, fruit smoothies, chai tea, cookie and cake mixes—you name it. And I had found my way into this amazing opportunity because I was looking to fix our margin and space problems with my first business.

YOU CAN BE THE BEST

Sometimes finding a way means you have to get creative and do something strange and maybe even a little risky—like starting a whole new second business to become a customer of the first. The "way" isn't always obvious or easy, but if you look for it, you can find it.

DON'T LET FEAR PREVENT YOU
FROM TAKING ACTION

In my nearly four decades of entrepreneurship, I've met countless people who say they dream of launching their own business. But they never do it. Why? They're afraid to give up their comfortable jobs and steady paychecks, and who can blame them? They've worked hard to get into a comfortable job making a great salary with great benefits. They have a nice car in the driveway of a nice house and a couple of kids to care for. Life is good.

Though some of these would-be entrepreneurs are not excited about their day jobs, they're stuck because the security is too risky to give up. They're fearful of the unknown. They have a dream, but they're afraid of what they could possibly lose.

So when people ask me, "What does it take to start a business?" here's what I tell them.

If you really want to do this and you have a great idea for a company, be prepared to sacrifice. The first thing you should do is sit down with your family and say, "Hey, this is what I would like to do. It means making significant sacrifices over the next three or four years. But it has the potential to be highly successful." If you have a great idea to create something, whether it's a product or a service, you need to be willing to take some risks, because it's almost impossible to do in your spare time with only spare money.

Really, this advice applies to any big goal, not just starting a company. If there's something you want, you're going to have to make sacrifices. That's what finding a way means. It means using whatever you have—whether that's time, money, energy, creativity, or so on—to get what you want.

Finding a way also means you don't wait for opportunities to come to you. You take action to create your own success. As *The Golf Mystic* says, "Life happens, whether you're ready or not. All we have is the moment. Sometimes waiting for ready is not an option." If you spend all your time waiting to be "ready"—to feel like you're totally ready to take a big step or make a big change—that's never going to happen. None of us ever feels "ready." Don't wait for a certain feeling or a certain sign that it's time. Whether you're ready or not, take the leap and pursue your passion and goals.

Doing this can be uncomfortable, but that's simply what it takes. Don't like being uncomfortable? Then by all means, stay in the comfortable job. But if you can get past the fear of the unknown, then your dreams become more than dreams. They have a chance to become reality.

KEEP YOURSELF OPEN TO OPPORTUNITIES

Opportunities hit us smack in the face every day. But most people don't recognize it, even when the opportunity is right in front of them. I believe that only one person out of a hundred recognizes when an opportunity presents itself. I carry this theory even further. Of the 1 percent who see an opportunity, 99 percent will not act on it. To take advantage of opportunities, you have to keep your awareness level up and remain open to life's possibilities, and you must be willing to act.

People see my success in entrepreneurship, and they'll say to me, "I'd like to run my own business."

I always respond with, "What kind of company would you like to own?"

The response, almost every time, is: "Oh, I have no idea. I just want to own my own company!"

Can you imagine? They haven't thought about the type of business they want to start. They're only thinking about the rewards and benefits of owning a successful company—the lifestyle they think entrepreneurship will bring to them. They want the end result but have no clue as to what it really takes—they're focused on outcomes, not opportunities. Consequently, these people are the least likely to succeed.

When you own a business, you're committing to that business twenty-four hours a day, 365 days a year. There's no turning it off.

Your mind is constantly exploring the possibilities—the possibilities of what may go wrong, but also the many more possibilities for something to go right. There's a name for this type of 365/24/7 devotion to your business. It's called passion. You absolutely need to be passionate about your business in order to succeed.

This is why I talked so much earlier about the importance of passion. When you're passionate about something—be it a business or another goal—you immerse yourself in it, and you're more likely to see the opportunities. When I developed the idea for Pinnacle Food Products, it was because all of my waking hours were devoted to solving a problem we were facing with Priority Food Processing. By remaining open to possibility, I found the next opportunity, which not only solved our problem but laid the groundwork for our next stage of growth.

In addition to passion, you need that positivity I talked about in the previous chapter. In *The Golf Mystic*, Gary Battersby writes, "Keep plotting with an optimism that opens you up to whatever is possible. As you move forward, you must be open to possibilities. That is exactly what allows you to discover every day." When you mire yourself in negativity or pessimism, you're automatically shutting out so many discoveries and possibilities, whether you realize it or not. In order to see the opportunities, you must first believe they exist, and that starts with optimism. Approaching life and the world around you with unflappable positivity starts a cycle of opportunities and hopefulness that infuses your outlook and the outlooks of those around you. And I can tell you from experience that positivity will always win over negativity —always.

Opportunities and choices are at hand all the time. You simply need the passion and positivity to take advantage of them.

LIFE OWES YOU NOTHING

One of my favorite pieces of advice that I give golf mentees is this: "Golf owes you nothing." I find it ironic how golf owes me nothing—and yet I owe everything to golf. I wouldn't be the person I am today without golf. Without golf, I would have never become a caddie. And without caddying, I wouldn't have received a great high school education, nor would I have received a great college education at Indiana University from my Chick Evans Scholarship. Without caddying and a great education, I wouldn't have found my first job opportunity, which led me to starting two great companies. Over my lifetime, I've made more than five hundred friends just through golf. And golf has taught me innumerable lessons over the years—about persistence and humility and the value of hard work.

I also love this advice because you can swap out *golf* for just about anything. For my father, you could say *America*. America didn't owe him anything, but he owes everything to America. It's because he came to the United States that he met my mother, his heaven on earth, and was able to start a family, which was always his proudest accomplishment.

The point of this advice is that everything is an opportunity, nothing more. You aren't guaranteed certain results. Your career owes you nothing. Other people owe you nothing. *Life* owes you nothing. There is one thing and one thing only that owes you something: *you*.

I say I owe everything to golf, but in truth, I owe it to myself. I'm the one who snuck on the golf course when I couldn't afford the green fees. I'm the one who worked to become the best caddie I could become. I'm the one who started my businesses. Likewise, while America opened up new paths for my father, he is the one who chose to immigrate and take advantage of those opportunities.

If you expect something from the world around you, you will almost always be disappointed. Instead, recognize that life owes you nothing, so whatever you want out of this life, it's up to you to find a way to achieve it.

CHAPTER 6

BE HONEST AND TRUSTING

MY FATHER, ZIGGY, was an extremely honest person. Some people are only honest when other people are looking, because they're worried about their reputation. My father held himself to a higher standard. He believed in moral integrity, and he followed his moral compass even when it wasn't to his advantage.

Before he found work as a meat cutter at Swift and Company, my father worked low-paid janitorial jobs. One day while emptying trash bins and cleaning the floors, he found a $20 bill laying on the ground. This was in the early 1950s. At the time, the windfall would have been the equivalent of two weeks' wages.

Many people would have pocketed the $20. Two weeks' wages goes a long way towards covering rent or buying groceries. My father was struggling to survive, and finding $20 on the ground might have seemed like divine intervention. But he knew the money belonged to someone, and there was no way he could take what wasn't his. He did what was right in his mind and turned the money in.

"Wow, Ziggy, this is very commendable you did this," his boss said. "Tell you what. I'm going to hang onto this, and if no one comes looking for it over the next week, I'm going to give it to you."

A week later no one came in to claim the $20 bill, and my father's boss gave it to him as a reward for his honesty.

Honesty and integrity were values my parents taught us kids. Unfortunately for us, we didn't come by these values easily. The one and only time I stole anything was from my father, and it left me with a feeling of shame and guilt for many years after.

When my maternal grandfather died, a collection of old coins was found in his basement, and my father kept them for safekeeping in a secret hiding place in our home. The collection included silver dollars, half dollars, quarters, and dimes dating from the late 1800s and early 1900s.

My older brother Rich was about nine years old when he discovered the stash of old coins in a big chest by our parents' bed. He began taking the coins, piece by piece, and one day he showed me the coins, and I began to take some also, our crime never going noticed by either of our parents. In our child minds we didn't think we were stealing. We didn't understand that these coins were special and valuable, and we thought we'd pay our father back with the money we made delivering newspapers, cutting grass, etc. This is what we thought, but let's face it: we were stealing.

Hundreds of silver coins were stashed in that chest. Over time, we probably swiped nearly half. Eventually, our father discovered the theft, and our mother knew right away who the culprits were. My brother and I were taking a bath together in our one-bathroom house, and in stormed our father, belt in hand, along with our mother. "Kill 'em, Ziggy, kill 'em, Ziggy!" my mother screamed. She was more upset than my dad—they were her father's coins. "Kill 'em!" she shouted again. My brother and I were stuck in that tub, and we sure took our whipping. (My mother's words might come across harshly on the page, but obviously she did not want our father to kill us. It just gives you an idea of what a big deal our theft was to her and my dad.)

Our whipping was a hard, painful lesson—but even more painful was the hurt my brother and I had caused our parents. We had failed my father twice. First, by stealing from him and breaking his trust in us. And secondly, by failing to follow his example. He was the type of person who couldn't fathom pocketing a $20 bill found on the ground. The fact that we took something that wasn't ours made him and my mom furious. Even as I got older, I couldn't revisit that memory without feeling enormous regret. It was like a scar. We were so stupid.

My parents were loving people, and they forgave us not long after discovering our thefts. But the memory of how we hurt them—and the awful feeling of guilt and shame—was something I felt for a very long time.

Though painful, the lesson was very valuable. And while it was my first and most impactful lesson in being honest, it was far from the last. Throughout my life, I've learned several lessons about honesty and trust. Life and success ultimately come down to relationships, and relationships are built on honesty and trust. So these lessons are maxims to live by.

LESSON #1: YOUR WORD IS EVERYTHING

If you take away only one thing from this chapter, let it be this: your word is everything. If you say you're going to do something, do it. If people can't trust your words, they can't trust you.

I learned this lesson from George Lauritzen, who taught me his word didn't matter—not even if you had a signed contract in hand.

Our problems with Pillsbury began when George wouldn't keep his word. They came to us with a new, nationwide product, and our sales guy mistakenly quoted and signed a contract for a price far below cost. The error was wholly our own. Instead of honoring the contract, George fought tooth and nail with Pillsbury. In the end, Pillsbury wrote George a big check to make him financially whole, and then they took their business to someone they could trust.

With me too, George proved not to be a man of his word.

Following the fiasco with Pillsbury, I hit the pavement and worked my butt off turning the company around. I did that because George promised me a $60,000 salary and an ownership stake. I never got either. This dishonesty was a big factor in my decision to quit.

After my experience with George, I vowed to be a different kind of business owner and person. My word became gospel. It was everything to me. I believed that if I wanted to run a great company, my word would need to be golden. If I said to one of my employees, "Hey, you're going to get a salary increase," or "You're going to get a bonus," then that person got an increase in pay or a bonus. It was done. Signed, sealed, and delivered. People knew, "This guy will never lie to us. He will never cheat us. He will always protect us from an employment standpoint." There was never an employee in my thirty-five years that ever said, "John didn't keep his word."

And guess what—my employees were incredible! They were hardworking and deserved every single raise they got. When you're honest with people, they will respect and appreciate you. Being honest is one of the most fundamental qualities of human decency.

We've all had our experiences with dishonest people. When another person behaves dishonestly towards you, it actually makes you feel anxiety. You're in a situation where someone is trying to take advantage of you or has lied to you. And that's a very difficult thing for both of you to overcome. Trust is an easy thing to lose, and a very hard thing to regain.

I don't think you can really be successful in business or life if you're not honest. The minute you do something dishonest, you risk it all. You head down a path that will only lead to personal destruction. When you're dishonest, your relationships can crumble like a house of cards. Everything you've built can be lost in a minute. Once you've been caught in a lie or acting in a way that is untrustworthy, no one will want to trust you again.

So whether it's in business or your personal life, it just pays to be honest. If you make a promise, keep it. Your word is everything.

LESSON #2: START WITH TRUST

For me, honesty is fundamentally about trust, and trust is a two-way street. In life, in addition to receiving trust (which you get by being honest), you will need to give trust as well.

There's two ways to go through life. You can be the type of person who makes others "earn" your trust, or you can trust people from day one.

I'm in the latter camp. I start with trust. I consider all people—even complete strangers—trustworthy until they prove otherwise. I think this has helped me in my journeys, in all areas of my life. I've developed so many great friendships because I was open to meeting new people and I didn't make someone earn my trust first.

What does this say about my belief in human beings? It means I believe we're all naturally good-hearted people who deserve each other's respect and trust. It means I believe we all should be given a chance to show how great we are—and it's only a handful of people who will show themselves to be untrustworthy.

Maybe this has happened to you. Let's say you're at a gathering, such as a conference or a party, and you meet a total stranger. Something in their mannerisms tells you they might not be a good person, or maybe you've heard this from someone else. You think, "Should I really be talking with this person?" Your defenses go up. But then you find yourself chatting, and you discover, "This person is really, really nice. Why was I afraid to speak with them?" I would say that 95-plus percent of the time, people turn out to be pretty nice if you give them the chance. It's only a small percentage of people who will disappoint you.

You could live life the other way, but it's a difficult, lonely path. Not trusting people from the outset means you will inevitably make fewer friends. If you require someone to earn your trust before really engaging with them, it means you would never engage with a stranger. Even with acquaintances, you will put up walls and keep them at a distance. You won't be able to have the kinds of conversations that lead to connection. The irony is that by requiring people to earn your trust, you never give them the chance to do exactly that!

I can't tell you how many friendships I've developed over the years that grew from a conversation with a complete stranger. My friendship with Lilia Vu started with one stranger asking another about her golf swing. If she didn't trust me—or if I didn't feel comfortable talking with her—then she and I would have never accomplished what we've done together and built our fabulous friendship!

I get it—trust is difficult. Most of us were taught as children not to trust strangers. Most of us also know what it feels like to have our trust broken, and it hurts. We close ourselves off and keep our guard up so we don't get hurt again. Here's the thing: if you go through life not trusting anyone, you are the one you're hurting. It might feel like you're protecting yourself, but really, you're limiting yourself. You're trying to avoid pain instead of trying to achieve happiness.

Trusting others means letting go of control, and that is scary, but it can also have big rewards. Consider George Lauritzen again. He never figured out how to trust others. Aside from his broken promises, the other reason I quit was his constant backseat driving and nitpicking. After he blew up the Pillsbury account, he asked me to help save the company, which is exactly what I did, bringing in more than fifty new customers. But it wasn't enough for him. He had to be at the center of everything and couldn't trust me to do my job.

Imagine if George had stepped back and let me continue to grow the business. When I left Lauritzen and Company, I started Priority Food Processing and grew it from scratch into a $10 million-a-year business. If I could do that starting from

BE HONEST AND TRUSTING

nothing, imagine what I could have done with Lauritzen and Company, which was doing about $2.5 million per year when I left. It already had a plant, tons of equipment, and employees. With those resources, there's no doubt I could have grown Lauritzen and Company into a $20 million-a-year (or more!) business, if George had simply put his faith and trust in the person he trained.

But it wasn't in his nature. He couldn't let go of control. Don't be like George. If you go through life withholding trust, then you're going to eliminate hundreds of great possibilities. You'll end up closing yourself off to relationships and opportunities that make life so interesting and richly rewarding. So don't make people earn trust; give it to them by default.

LESSON #3: NEVER TRUST A GOLF CHEAT

Recently someone asked me why I loved golf so much. "What's so special about it?" they asked.

With golf, you're on your own. You don't have teammates to blame when your game goes south. With sports such as football, basketball, baseball, or hockey, it's a game of physical toughness—there's always someone after you, ready to hit you hard. But with golf, it's just you against this little ball that just waits and waits for you to hit it and move it towards your target. It's a game played in your head as much as it's played on the green. Because of all this, you can learn a lot about a person by watching how they play golf.

Golf also has a way of exposing people for who they really are. The other thing that's truly special about golf is that there are no referees, no umpires. In every other sport I can think of, players do everything in their power to get away with breaking the rules or cheating. That's why they need referees and umpires, to catch them.

In golf, if you break a rule, you're supposed to call it on yourself. That's the beauty of the game—a tradition of etiquette, honesty, respect, and honor.

Now, does that mean every golfer is honest? Of course not! Many golfers allow their ego to get in the way. They'll lie about their scores, to make it seem like they're better than they really are. You might ask them, "What did you score on that hole?" And they'll say five when they really shot a six. They won't call penalties on themselves and might even move their ball out of a tough spot if no one's looking.

Now, here's the real irony. In golf, there is a handicap system which allows players of different abilities to compete against each other. A golfer who lies about their ability will have a lower handicap, which makes it more difficult for them to win! Some other golfers do the opposite and give themselves a higher handicap than their actual ability, to help them win. Both types of golfers are only cheating themselves because deep inside they are being dishonest. Neither of them will ever achieve the true joy and success the game brings to countless others.

This applies beyond golf as well. Dishonesty is typically a short-cut. It's often a way to get something without truly earning it. It's the difference between having a helicopter drop you off at the top of a mountain versus hiking up yourself. In both, you can stand on the summit, but only with the latter do you build the muscles and stamina to climb more mountains in the future. So while it can be tempting to take dishonest shortcuts in life, you're just hurting yourself in the long run, because you're depriving yourself of all the skills and growth that come from hard work. You're also going to damage your self-esteem. All those golfers who lie about their scores? They know they're lying. They know that it's all a facade and they're not as good as they say. I'm guessing they probably don't look too closely at themselves in the mirror each day. Real confidence, personal satisfaction, and self-esteem come from knowing you earned your achievements.

How someone behaves on the golf course will most likely mirror how they behave off the course. So I always say this: if a person cheats at golf, you can be quite certain you don't want to do business with them off the course. They don't respect you—or themselves—enough to be honest. Someone who is willing to lie in a game, because of ego issues or a lack of self-esteem, will lie to you in business too. Bottom line: if you can't trust a person on the green, you can't trust them with your green either.

Now you might be thinking, "John, I don't play golf!" The real point of this lesson isn't about golf. It's that when someone

shows you who they are, you should believe them. I advise starting with trust, but when someone behaves dishonestly, you take
that trust away. And don't assume you'll be the exception to the
rule. If someone is willing to lie and cheat others, why wouldn't
they do the same to you? So pay attention to others' dishonesty,
whether it's fudging the rules on the golf course, talking badly
about others behind their back, or a company cutting corners to
improve their margins.

LESSON #4: BE HONEST EVEN WHEN IT'S HARD

Most people consider themselves honest, and I agree. Most people
are honest most of the time. However, very few people are honest
all of the time. Every single lesson in this book is "easy," right up
until it's not. The measure of your honesty is how you act when
it gets difficult—like when you find $20 that could really help
your family.

Honesty is difficult when (1) being dishonest will help you
gain something (whether it's money, prestige, etc.) or (2) being
honest will be uncomfortable.

For the first, remember the big picture. When I was running
my companies, I was always honest not just with my employees,
but with my customers and vendors too. If we had a key ingredient
drop in cost—say, for example, sugar or cocoa powder—we would
lower prices for our customers before they even asked. We'd say,

"You know what, our costs have come down, so we're going to take seventy-five cents off your case of cappuccino or hot chocolate."

We didn't have to do this. We could have just kept quiet and raked in some extra profit. But that still would have been dishonest in my mind, and I wasn't thinking about our profits for the quarter; I was thinking about our profits over the lifetime of the business. Rather than making extra money short term, I wanted to build strong, trusting relationships with these customers for the long term. How often do businesses offer to lower prices like this? Almost never! (I'm not talking about promotions and discounts here, which are sales tactics, but true price adjustments.) That proactive gesture goes a long way to helping you stand out against the competition. Your customers remember you for it.

But something else happens. Good gestures flow back in your direction. In the future there were times when our ingredient and raw materials costs went up, and I went to the client and said, "We need to increase our selling price by fifty cents per case, because our costs have gotten higher." They remembered how we had reduced prices in the past, and they accepted an increase without complaint. They said, "Okay, no problem, John. Have it be effective from the first of the month." There wasn't any argument, because our clients trusted us and they knew we were true partners in business together.

If the client absolutely didn't want to pay the higher price, we gave them another option, which they rarely took. We could lower costs by reengineering their formula, substituting one ingredient for something less expensive. Nine times out of ten our clients said, "You know what? We don't want our product changed. We'll take the price increase." They didn't want to compromise on quality, so they absorbed the increase.

But ingredient substitution is a common form of dishonesty many food companies practice today, especially amid high inflation, and it always leaves a bad taste in my mouth when I see this practice. Instead of using a twelve-dollar flavor, a big brand company might switch to an eight-dollar flavor. A little bit of dishonesty for the sake of easy profit. The change is subtle, but the company is relying on the power of its brand in the hopes that you, the consumer, won't notice. What happens is these substitutions accumulate over time, until one day the product is a poor imitation of the original. You have a second-rate product, and pretty soon you have a second-rate company too. This is why when I got into the business of making our own cappuccino and gourmet chocolate, I always insisted on the best ingredients. It was a form of honesty you could literally taste.

You're going to face difficult situations and conversations in life. It could be giving someone feedback at work, talking to a friend about something they did that hurt you, or having to break bad news to someone. Honesty can feel painful in the moment, but in the long run, dishonesty is a disservice to both you and the other person. All you're really doing is letting problems fester.

You will have to face the problem eventually, and it's better to do it sooner rather than later, as problems tend to escalate the longer they're avoided.

I do find it necessary to mention that the world is not black and white. I think we should strive to be honest always, but there are exceptions to every rule. You could find yourself in a situation in which you need to lie for your safety or when telling the truth would be unnecessarily hurtful to others. But if you find yourself leaning towards dishonesty for selfish benefit, then you're helping no one. It's better to be frank, open, and truthful.

DO BETTER

One Christmas, after I had achieved some success in business, I went around to every coin dealer I could find in Chicago to try to rebuild my father's coin collection. I spent several thousands of dollars on silver dollars, half dollars, quarters, and dimes. I put these in a big velvet bag and gave them to my father as a Christmas present. It was my way of saying, "I never forgot what we did, and I want you to know just how sorry I am!"

My father had already long forgiven me at that point, but that gift meant a lot to him. It wasn't about the coins themselves—it had never been about the coins. It was about honesty. I was showing him that I'd learned my lesson and was working to do better.

As I know firsthand, dishonesty can stick with you for a long time. None of us are perfect human beings. Trust me, I'm not, you're not. You will make mistakes. What matters is how you own up to them. You may not always be able to correct your mistakes, like I did with the coins, but you can always learn from them. It's never too late to start being honest and doing better.

CHAPTER 7

BE KIND

I'VE ALWAYS KNOWN my father to be a fundamentally good person. But there's one story in particular—more than any of the other stories I know about the man—that has left an indelible impression on me and helped me to understand the kind of human being my father really was. It's a story from his time as a prisoner of war, when he was confronted with a horrible, unthinkable choice.

One day while he and some fellow prisoners of war were working on a nearby farm, they ran across a group of armed German soldiers abusing a Jewish woman.

"You, come over here," the soldiers ordered my father.

My father did as he was told. He knew what happened if you didn't follow orders. He had seen mass graves filled with bodies and understood his existence was precarious and day-to-day.

The soldiers shoved a rifle into his shaking hands. "Shoot her," they commanded.

My father didn't move.

"If you don't shoot her, we will shoot you," the soldiers said.

In that moment, my father thought, *I'm going to die.* Because he knew he could never pull the trigger. Taking the life of an innocent woman to save his own wasn't something he could even think of doing. All he could do was say a silent prayer on what he thought would be the last day of his life.

Literally seconds after saying his silent prayers, air raid sirens went off. The Allies were dropping bombs onto the neighboring areas. The stunned German soldiers grabbed the rifle back from my father and took off running. My father and the woman were spared their lives.

My father believed those bombs were an act of God—a miracle. I believe there were actually two miracles that day. The bombs were the second. The first was my father, choosing not to shoot the woman, even if it meant he had to die. Anyone who was lucky enough to have met and spent time with Ziggy knows what I know: he would have taken the bullet rather than shoot that innocent woman.

Can you even imagine being in that position, forced to choose between your own life and another's? I think many would choose to shoot the woman to stay alive. But not my dad. He didn't have an ounce of hate in him or the ability to hurt others. Taking the life of an innocent woman to save his own wasn't something he could even think of doing. He chose to do the right thing, and he was saved.

When my dad shared this story with my older sister Mimi many years ago, he cried, and when Mimi recently shared the story with me, it also brought tears to my eyes. Had things gone just a little differently that day—if the bombs had fallen just a minute later than they did—my father would have died. None of my siblings or I would even exist. I've always known my father to be a good man, but this story magnified for me just how extraordinary a human being he really was. It also gave new meaning to one of the lessons he taught me: be kind! For my father, that wasn't a superficial platitude, but a deep philosophy about life.

IF YOU CAN'T SAY SOMETHING GOOD...

Being kind doesn't have to be as extreme as sacrificing your life for another. It can be as simple and easy as keeping your mouth shut. Something Ziggy often told us kids—and that your parents probably taught you too—is if you can't say anything good about someone, don't say anything at all. Now, there is some nuance here. This advice doesn't mean you have to ignore or tolerate people's bad behavior. But you need to distinguish between being truthful and being hurtful. It comes down to your intention: Are you saying something because it can be helpful or needs to be said, or because you want to tear someone else down?

You should avoid tearing other people down not only for their sake, but for your own. People who say mean or unkind things about others tend to have something in common: they're not happy. They're filled with negativity. Instead of seeing the good in people and the world, they zero in on the bad and start complaining. Often, when they feel the need to trash someone else, it's often because they feel small. There's something lacking in their own life, and they try to make themselves feel better by bringing someone else down.

This is no way to live life. Tearing someone else down does not actually lift you up, so any satisfaction you gain from it will be temporary and fleeting. When you voice unkind thoughts aloud, you're just feeding into negativity, reinforcing your own unhappiness. And personally, when someone talks badly about another person, I almost always end up thinking more poorly of the person doing the talking than the person being talked about.

It seems counterintuitive, but the first step in being kind is to focus not on others, but on yourself—specifically, on your mindset. Whenever you feel the inclination to say something mean or unkind about a person, stop and ask yourself why. Ask yourself, "What is it that I am thinking or feeling that's causing me to have these negative thoughts?" Focus on trying to get rid of the negativity, not only so you can treat others more kindly, but also so you can be happier.

Negativity breeds negativity, so also be careful about who you surround yourself with. I'm always especially surprised when people gossip and talk badly about supposed friends behind their backs. I've never kept friends like this around, because I can't help thinking, "When I'm not here, do they talk this way about me too?" I wouldn't be able to trust those friends completely. If I left for a moment, maybe for the bathroom, and came back to smirks and sideways glances, I'd start wondering. Did I miss a joke, or was I the joke? That doubt and insecurity could eat away at me.

In every interaction, you have the choice to approach it with positive or negative energy. Negativity can become a habit, but the more you learn to recognize it (in yourself and in others), the more you can begin shifting towards positivity. The more positive you are, the happier—and more successful—you will be, and the easier it will be for you to be kind to others.

MEAN GUYS FINISH LONELY

Being kind really isn't that hard, yet many people resist it. They think you have to be at least a little bit mean to get ahead and be successful in life. My first boss George Lauritzen was like that. For him, being mean was a point of pride. I kid you not, the man kept a plaque on his office door that said: "George F. Lauritzen, Chairman of the Board, a real mean miserable son of a bitch. Nice guys finish last. May his tribe increase."

George Lauritzen was an old-school entrepreneur—the last of a dinosaur breed. He believed the only way to win was to be tough and even mean if necessary. I'm here to tell you, George

Lauritzen was wrong. It's a silly notion that nice guys finish last. A small percentage of mean guys might indeed finish first, but they also finish lonely, with no one meaningful in their life to celebrate their achievements.

Many successful people will say, "It's lonely at the top," but that's probably because they were like George Lauritzen and weren't very nice to people along the way. For me, success has been anything but lonely. I find myself at the end of a thirty-five-year career surrounded by the warmth of hundreds of friendships, some of which I've had since kindergarten. These are people who've truly enriched my life, whom I share a deep and meaningful connection with. I might not see some of them for many years, but when we get back together, it's like no time has passed. It's always, "Let's get lunch or dinner together! Let's play golf! Let's do this and that! It's so wonderful to see you!"

I've been very blessed with an abundance of friendship specifically because I prioritize kindness. Whether it's with family members, the people that I've worked with, or even strangers I've just met, I always try to bring a positive energy and kindness into my interactions with people.

Here's the thing: in both business and life, people have options. They don't have to work with you or hang out with you. Negative people aren't very fun to be around. If you've ever witnessed an angry customer berate a poor retail employee over something inconsequential, I bet you didn't think, *I want to be friends with that person.* You probably thought, *What a jerk!* If you're an awful person to be around, people will go somewhere else. George learned this the hard way when Pillsbury took its business elsewhere, and he learned it when I decided to quit the company.

In contrast, people are drawn to kindness. When you treat everyone well, people want to hang out with you. I talked earlier about how positivity will make you a happier person, but the really great thing about positivity is that it's infectious. When you're positive and happy, the people around you become positive and happy too. So it not only helps you, it helps others.

You don't have to go through life on the mistaken notion that nice guys finish last. Remember that success isn't about dollars. It's about overall happiness, and in the currency of happiness, friendships are like million-dollar bills to me. In that way, mean guys finish poor and lonely, while nice guys finish with true wealth.

THE THREE-LEGGED STOOL OF BUSINESS AND WHAT IT MEANS TO TREAT PEOPLE WELL

Success isn't about dollars, but if money is important to you, you're still better off treating people well than being "a real mean miserable son of a bitch." That was my policy at my companies, and it made a big difference—about a $7.5 million difference (how much more my first company was worth compared to Lauritzen and Company).

I've met hundreds of would-be entrepreneurs who have sought advice on how to launch and run a successful company. I've spoken at business schools, and I've given talks about both running a business and starting one. The students come looking for some secret insight, some nugget of information that can give them an extra edge.

The advice I have to give them is actually very simple: treat people well. This very simple idea is how I grew Priority Food Processing and Pinnacle Food Products to become the best in their industries.

More specifically, a successful business needs to treat three groups well: its employees, its customers, and its suppliers. Think of it as a three-legged stool. If any one leg is missing, the company is never going to be great. If two legs are missing, the company will most likely not succeed. And if all three legs are missing, well, you're basically doomed. A lot of companies have two legs, but rarely do companies hit the trifecta.

It's a win-win-win approach to doing business. And while this advice is framed from the perspective of someone running a company, there are also broader lessons here that can apply to any career or your personal life. Think about it: if you have aspirations of becoming a singer, you want to treat your agent well, your music producer well, your fans well. All three are partners in your success. So even if you don't have any desire to be an entrepreneur or run a business, understanding how a business should treat its employees, customers, and suppliers will tell you a lot about how you should treat people in your life.

Leg #1: Treat Your Employees Well

In order to have a great company, you need to have great employees. And in order to attract and keep great employees, you need to treat them well.

Treating our employees well was always a top priority for me. Everyone says they have the best employees, but in my case, I know it was true. My companies grew to have about 250 positions, and we had extremely low turnover in thirty-five years. Because we treated people well, they stayed with us. Many spent their entire careers with us and retired with us.

The way to treat employees well is the same as treating anyone well: treat them with dignity and respect.

At a company, respect comes across in the language you use and how you address people. First, I never once in thirty-five years said that an employee worked "for" me. Our employees didn't work for me; we worked with each other. There's a fundamental difference between the two, and if you're someone who employs people, I'd advise you to think about how the former of those two phrases asserts authority, while the latter gives an employee respect and promotes a sense of unity.

The life lesson here is to not think of yourself as better than anyone else. Treat everyone as your equal.

"Working with each other" was more than just words for me. While I owned the companies, I didn't shy away from the "dirty work." I dumped powders, bagged and cased them, drove the forklift, participated in product development, and more. As the companies grew, I naturally spent more time doing the work of leadership as opposed to the day-to-day work on the factory floor. But I never forgot what it was like to do all those different jobs, and it made me appreciate and respect the people working with me that much more.

The life lesson? Put yourself in other people's shoes so that you can better understand their challenges and needs.

I also made it a point to learn every single employee's name and greet them when I walked through the plant. When we had 250 positions, that was a lot of names! But since our turnover was so low, getting to know everyone individually was not as hard as you'd imagine. Saying "Good morning, Francisco!" and "Hey, Irene, how are you doing?" is such an easy thing to do. Even when people were new to our company, I would address them by name. I often saw this surprised look on their face that said, "Wow! The owner of this company knows my name?" Think about what that simple gesture does for people. It tells them that you value them as a person, not just as an employee. I knew their names because they all meant something to me, and that meant something to them.

This is something you can do outside of the business world too.

If there are people you interact with regularly—maybe a barista at your favorite coffee shop or a neighbor or an employee at your golf club—make an effort to learn and remember their name.

Another thing I did at my companies was give people raises or bonuses to acknowledge their hard work—before they even thought to ask. One of the hardest things to do is to go to your boss and say, "Hey, I feel I really deserve a raise." It's an awkward conversation. Asking for a raise can be a very tough and emotional situation for an employee, and many people don't get paid what they deserve because they're afraid of that encounter. A hard-working but shy employee might be earning far less than the value they contribute.

A great company will proactively recognize and reward its employees. I made it a policy at my companies that employees wouldn't have to ask for a pay increase. I always took care of them first. In my thirty-five years, I only had one person walk into my office and ask for a raise. (And tellingly, that was the one person who didn't really deserve one.) There's no greater way to recognize an employee than to reward them financially before they even expect it.

In life, a "raise" or "bonus" could mean doing extra chores for your spouse, taking a friend out to dinner, buying a family member a small surprise gift—anything that shows your appreciation. If you do such things proactively, the gesture will be even more meaningful, because you're showing the person it's something you

YOU CAN BE THE BEST

want to do because you appreciate them, not something you're doing out of a sense of obligation.

One of the biggest lessons I learned as an employer is that, whether it's business or life, people are people. If you treat them well and with respect, they will want to give it right back to you—and to others too. Treating people well creates a culture of kindness and respect. The people you treat well will go on to treat other people in their life well.

Leg #2: Treat Your Customers Well

In a business, treating your customers well should be obvious. Every business book and class teaches this, and if they don't, ask for a refund. Revenue and profit are the lifeblood of a company. To bring in revenue and make a profit, you need to take care of your customers.

There are various ways a company can service its customers. For us, it was right there in the name of my first company, Priority Food Processing. We let our customers know they were our top priority. We worked really hard to communicate with our clients to make sure we were fulfilling all their needs. We treated them with honesty, and we were passionate and enthusiastic about their business. We loved making our customers truly pleased with everything we did to help them succeed. When customers and suppliers came through our front door, they immediately saw in big letters on the wall: "Partners in Success."

Much of treating your customers well is creating a work environment where taking care of others is the ethos underlying all your interactions. Taking care of your employees reinforces your ability to take care of your customers. When you make your employees a priority, they in turn will make your company and your customers their priority.

In a broader sense, your "customers" are all the people who add value to your life—the people who bring you happiness, whoever provides you with a livelihood, those who offer a listening ear, and so on. It's important that you not take these people for granted, because they are critical to your success and well-being. At the same time, remember: treating people well doesn't apply just to those who provide value to you. The ultimate success—happiness and contentment—can only be achieved when you treat *everyone* well, when you always show kindness and generosity to others.

Leg #3: Treat Your Suppliers Well

This is the third leg of the stool, and for some reason, it's the leg that is most often missing. Only the greatest of companies do it: treat your suppliers well.

Taking care of your suppliers is usually the missing link to an incredible business. I always used to say, "Win. Win. Win. Everybody has to win." The customers—obviously, they have to win. Your employees, they have to win. But your suppliers have to win also. And if everyone wins, guess what? You win, and your company can become truly great—not just good, but the best company it can possibly be.

You're probably thinking, "Why should I treat my suppliers well? Aren't I their customer? They should be the ones treating me well." The answer is the same reason why you should treat your employees well. If you treat your suppliers well, they will go the extra mile to service your needs, which in turn helps you service your customers' needs and keep their business, which then means your suppliers keep your business. It's all intertwined. And it will be very powerful when all three legs are in place.

We didn't treat our suppliers as though we were their customers. We treated them as our clients. Once a year on a Friday in August, we'd host a big event for our suppliers at the Arlington Park racetrack. We'd gather under a huge tent down on the concourse for a day of horse racing, catered food, drinks, and camaraderie. Only suppliers were invited. Normally, you think of companies hosting that type of event for its clients. We did it for our suppliers, to show our appreciation and to let them know they were very much a part of our success.

On the following Monday, my phone would be ringing off the hook with supplier after supplier after supplier calling me up to say, "Hey, John, I just wanted to thank you for an amazing time on Friday. That has never happened in my entire business life, where a customer pulled in all the suppliers together and treated them to a day of entertainment. We called it "A Day at the Races."

We held the event every year for twenty years, until Insight Beverages was sold.

One of the greatest compliments I ever received in my business career came from our suppliers. They would say, "You know, John, you're our favorite company to call on." I'm sure that was because whenever a supplier visited, we never made them just sit in the lobby, like I did at Nestlé in White Plains all those years ago. They were invited into our conference room immediately, greeted with coffee or refreshments and friendly faces, and accorded respect. We treated our suppliers as one of our "partners in success."

It's easy to treat someone well when you are expected to or when you care deeply about them. But when kindness is not expected—like with suppliers, or a stranger on your commute, or the cashier at the grocery store—it becomes even more meaningful and rewarding. Treat people well when they don't expect it, and they will remember you for it.

The three-legged stool is a simple but very powerful formula: treat your employees well, treat your customers well, treat your suppliers well. When you do all three right, they work powerfully together to make not just a good company, but a great company. And all the fundamental principles behind how to treat those people right apply to life in general too. Just as you can't have a great company without great employees, customers, and suppliers, you can't have a great life without great relationships. So treat people great!

KILL THEM WITH KINDNESS, BUT
KNOW YOUR BOUNDARIES

When you're interacting with positive, good people, it's easy to be kind. It gets a whole lot harder when you're dealing with less than nice people who treat you poorly. It can be tempting to lash out and fight fire with fire, but if you really want to put out a fire, more fire isn't going to do you any good. You need water.

This is something Lilia experienced. When she first started playing on the LPGA, some of the other players were not very friendly. It's professional sports, with six-figure purses to be won. People can be pretty rough out there at times.

Coming back to the tour two and half years later, Lilia felt some apprehension about possibly seeing some of the non-friendly competitors again. I said to her, "This is what you do: kill them with kindness. Someone says something bad to you, just reply with kindness. They'll hate it. It will drive them crazy. If you just reply to them with kindness, they won't know what to do." This is something Ziggy taught me too. He would always say, "If someone throws stones, you throw bread." When you kill someone with kindness, there's no way they can knock you down. There's nothing they can do or say to harm you, because you're not playing their game.

Killing people with kindness should always be your go-to move, but it doesn't mean you let people walk all over you. You can be kind and still hold boundaries.

Earlier, I told you the story of how I started Priority Food Processing by piecing together a loan from my parents, a loan from a client, and a loan from a bank—$15,000 at 2 percentage points above prime. I was very grateful to the bank that was willing to work with a twenty-five-year-old, as-yet-unproven entrepreneur.

I worked hard to pay down that loan. I didn't want all my profits to be eaten up by interest. Within eighteen months, I had the principal down to $11,000. The Federal Reserve had also cut the prime rate by five percentage points, so that provided a tiny amount of relief as well. My interest fell from 23 percent to 18 percent.

After eighteen months of solid payments, I went to the bank to speak to the loan officer. I said, "Kate, I've done pretty well paying down this loan. I'd like you to consider giving me one percentage point above prime."

She said, "No, we can't do that."

While I was sitting with her, showing my disappointment on my face, I was glancing over my loan document, and for some reason my eyes caught something in the document I had never seen before. According to this paperwork, my loan now had a 17 percent floor clause. They had added this in without telling me, and it meant I would be stuck paying 17 percent, no matter how low rates fell. I said, "Kate, does this mean what I think it does? If prime goes down to thirteen, you still want me to pay seventeen?"

She nodded. "That's what we're doing with all our clients."

YOU CAN BE THE BEST

I said, "You know, I am very grateful to this bank for giving me a shot eighteen months ago when no one else would. And I will be loyal to your bank forever, but this is not fair. If you can't work with me on this, I will have to go look for another bank."

Without flinching, she said, "Go ahead. Find another bank."

Talk about a huge slap in the face! I was going to be loyal to this bank forever. But loyalty wasn't something they valued. So I found a new bank, one that gave me one percentage point above prime, which I believed was fair. Eighteen months later, this new bank provided me a personal loan for $125,000 to buy out my client's 49 percent interest in Priority Food Processing. I kept my business at that bank for the next twenty-eight years. All of my revolving credit facilities were at that bank, millions of dollars in loans that generated hundreds of thousands of dollars in interest for them.

I am a big believer in repaying kindness with kindness and even repaying meanness with kindness. But you have to know your boundaries. If someone is treating you unfairly, you owe it to yourself to change that relationship. And that brings us to our final, and very important, lesson of the chapter.

BE KIND TO YOURSELF

Being kind isn't just about treating others well. You are a person too, and you should treat yourself well.

It's important to be kind to yourself, because if you're not kind to yourself, how can you be kind to others? You've probably heard it a million times. You can't learn to love others until you learn to love yourself.

As *The Golf Mystic* says, "Self-love that allows a person to truly care for others shows they have a spirit that can't be broken." When we love ourselves and value ourselves, we automatically begin to love and value others. That valuation has an instant and automatic effect on our spirit and our approach to situations, experiences, and other people. When you truly love yourself, nothing anyone says or does can shake that, and as a result, your spirit is unbreakable. Problems no longer overwhelm because you know you have the tenacity to solve them. Difficult conversations no longer feel impossible because you know you value yourself and others enough to engage in saying and doing the hard things to reach the best resolution. Self-love is where it all starts, and once you experience that feeling, the rest will fall into place.

When I first started working with Luke, the thing I noticed about him, aside from his drive and intensity, was a certain lack of emotion. He had this idea that to be a tough competitor, you had to be almost stoic, which meant he never allowed himself to express much emotion while feeling the highs of winning or the lows of losing, except to be very hard on himself when things weren't going the way he wanted. I sensed he kept a lot of emotions bottled inside.

Luke played excellent golf in high school, became the best in the state, and was recruited on a scholarship to play college golf with a famous coach. Only for it to turn into disaster.

The coach ran a very results-focused program and didn't show compassion to the boys on his team. If you didn't deliver, he'd have very little to do with you. It was just about the worst environment possible for someone like Luke. Luke was already really hard on himself. Driven people are typically that way. They're not quick to reward themselves, but they're very quick to punish themselves when they don't do well. And now Luke had an external authority figure doing the same thing he was already doing to himself.

After four years, he graduated feeling disappointed, lacking confidence, and even worse, having lost some of his love for golf. When I started working with him, one of my first goals was to get him to start having fun and to express more of his emotions.

There's a real person inside everybody. We might try to hide that person behind a mask, but they're inside of us, and they need our kindness just as much as anyone else. If things don't turn out how you want, don't beat yourself up too much. Instead, actually start letting out some of your feelings, and start a journey of learning to love yourself.

A WHOLE LOT MORE COMPASSION

My father Ziggy had the biggest heart of anyone I know. He was constantly striking up conversations with people and trying to help others when he could. Compassion poured out of him into the world.

As a parent, I believe that if you teach your children to leave the house and go out into the world with a big heart, you've done your job. My parents did their job with me and my siblings, and I believe I have done that with my children.

Compassion is something I think we all could use more of these days. Compassion is what brings you relationships, and it's your relationships that bring you riches. I know I've always felt wealthier in friendships than I have in money.

We all have areas where we can be kinder and more compassionate—to ourselves and to others. Kindness doesn't cost you anything. It's not something you need to hold onto. It's meant to be given freely to others. So when given the choice between kindness and meanness, choose to be kind.

CHAPTER 8

BE GRATEFUL

I NEVER HEARD my father complain. Not once.

He had plenty he could have complained about. He spent the prime years of his life in the Polish army and as a prisoner of war. His life was precarious day-to-day, and there were many times he believed he wouldn't survive the war. After the war, when he came to America, he worked manual jobs, the kind that take a toll on your body and require a strength of mind.

But if anyone asked him—and even if they didn't ask him—he would tell them how blessed he was. When you've known true sorrow and hunger, true devastation and fear, you learn to recognize the joy and the value in the little things in life. For my father, his blessings mattered more than anything else. Instead of complaining, he was grateful. And in his eyes, he had a lot to be grateful for.

He was grateful for the German guard who came to like him, most likely due to his work ethic, and sometimes tossed him an extra potato.

He was grateful to be away from the camp and working on a farm the day when dozens of fellow POWs mysteriously disappeared, never to be seen or heard from again.

When the German soldiers ordered him to kill the Jewish woman, he was grateful for the sudden Allied bombing that saved him and her both.

He was grateful to God, who he believed saved him on more than one occasion, like when he was working in the fields one day and sliced open his hand on farm machinery. Blood gushed profusely from the wound. My father thought he was going to lose his hand. "God help me, I don't know what to do," he prayed. The loss of a hand was something he could survive, but if he wasn't able to work, how much longer would the German soldiers keep him alive?

Suddenly, out of a nearby wooded area came a trio of German nuns. They took him back to their monastery, and they sewed and bandaged up his hand. They saved his hand and perhaps his life, because he might have been killed had he not been able to work.

He was grateful the cramped, smelly boat didn't sink in the turbulent seas on the way to America. He was grateful a friend told him about the Polish community in Chicago, prompting his decision to leave New York City, which in turn led him to meet my mother, whom he considered his greatest blessing—the thing he was most grateful for.

He was grateful for every bite of food. When he was a prisoner of war, he never knew when he would eat next. He understood what it is to be hungry, so he never wasted food. In my entire life, I never once saw my dad leave food on his plate.

He was grateful for his job as a meat packer, even though it was a very tough job. It meant working in cold freezer conditions for hours at a time. One day, while cutting meat, his coworkers started shouting at him. "Ziggy! Ziggy! What's all that blood?" My father looked down to see the tip of his baby finger lying on the cutting table among the chunks of meat. He'd sliced it clean off, but it was so cold, his hands so numb, that he hadn't even felt it.

One Christmas break while I was home from college, I went to work alongside my father for a couple of weeks. I remember having to get up so early to start work at New City Meat Packing by seven every morning. My main job each day for eight hours was to break up large blocks of dry ice and wrap the pieces with packing paper for the meat packers to use with the gift boxes of steaks they mailed out each day. When I wasn't wrapping dry ice, I swept the floors. I remember saying to myself, "I don't ever want to do this for a living." But my father did do this for a living. He did it for thirty-five years, and he was grateful to be able to work and provide a living for his family.

I told you early in the book that my father is the most successful person I know, and that's directly connected to his gratefulness. Success—true success—cannot be measured externally. It is something internal, a feeling of satisfaction and pride in one's life. Being grateful and showing gratitude along your own journey to success is how you will become and feel like your very best self.

CULTIVATING GRATITUDE

I don't think we do enough to appreciate our blessings. Many people are unhappy and dissatisfied simply because they don't appreciate what they have and what they've achieved. We can cultivate gratitude in our lives by taking an inventory of the abundance in our lives.

As I've said before, success isn't about financial wealth. Money cannot buy happiness; it can only buy comfort. There is nothing wrong with comfort, but too many people get stuck in an endless cycle of acquiring material goods. The acquisition of stuff might make you feel good—but only temporarily. Soon enough those material goods become what they really are. Just things.

The solution isn't to keep acquiring more things, hoping that eventually we'll feel fulfilled. The secret to fulfillment is gratitude, and gratitude is simple: you need to want less and do more.

No matter where you fall on the wealth spectrum, there's always someone with far less and far more. One of the things that amazed me about my father is he had so little, yet he knew there were many others who had far less, and he was always giving help to whomever he could. Helping others was how he expressed gratitude for the blessings life had given him. From his perspective, his life was abundant and blessed. He constantly talked about how thankful he was for everything he had.

But again, this is about so much more than financial wealth. There's plenty else to be grateful for in life. If you have great family relationships or friends you can turn to in a moment of need, you should feel very grateful. Many people don't have that. Likewise, if you're in good health, you should feel grateful, because many aren't so fortunate. Even when life is difficult, we can find things to be grateful for, whether it's the people in our life who care about us or simply the next breath we take. Being grateful comes from having a level of awareness of the many ways in which our lives are abundant—and not getting wrapped up in things that simply don't matter.

Ultimately, gratitude is a choice. My father chose to count his blessings rather than dwell on the ways his life might have been unfair. You can choose to complain, or you can choose to be grateful. Which of those choices do you think is going to bring you more happiness and joy? I think the answer is quite simple. Be grateful.

FINDING GRATITUDE IN UNEXPECTED PLACES

As kids, I don't think we ever fully appreciate our parents. It's not until we're older that we begin to comprehend the full dimensions of their lives—the richness of their experiences and their histories. In my father's case, his life was filled with trials and horrors he rarely spoke about. The extraordinary events of my father's life have taught me how to be grateful and how to appreciate the blessings of my own life. I am eternally grateful for my father, Ziggy.

It's very easy for me to be grateful for my father. I can't imagine what my life would have been without him. He was such a good man, and just about everyone who came into contact with him was grateful for him. But the real test of gratitude is learning how to find gratitude in unexpected places: in the challenges and difficulties of our lives.

There's another man who had an undeniable impact on my life. I've already told you a bit about him: George Lauritzen. Based on what you've already read, you know my experience with George wasn't the greatest, but you know what? I am so grateful for him.

When George hired me, he said if I went to work for him I'd learn everything about running a business. It was one of the major reasons I took the job. And you know what? He was right. I learned many valuable business lessons working at his company.

After George Lauritzen and I parted ways in 1980, we didn't speak or see each other for a long time. But about a decade later, I invited him to come see the operations at Priority Food Processing. George then was in his late seventies and had been retired for several years. I was in my mid-thirties and about to build our new state-of-the-art facility to bring all our locations under one roof.

I clearly remember giving George the grand tour of Priority Food Processing. It reminded me of that day back in 1977 when

I was fresh out of college and George invited me to his plant for a job interview. Back then, I didn't even know what inventory control was. Now here I was, with my own company and two hundred employees.

"Wow, this is really fantastic," George said to me. "You've done really well."

I could tell he was proud of what I had accomplished. George was famous for his gruffness, but as we spoke, there was something light and animated in his voice, as though we'd both been transported back in time.

"I had a good teacher," I kept reminding him. "I had a really good teacher."

A couple of years later, George passed away. I'm thankful I had that moment to shake his hand once more and bury the hatchet between us. I was grateful for the opportunity to acknowledge his role in my success, because I felt very blessed that he gave me a chance all those years ago. There weren't a lot of people back then willing to give a young college kid a shot, but George did. Running Lauritzen and Company at such a young age was an invaluable experience for me. It shaped me. It shaped what kind of businessman I wanted to become and who I wanted to be as a leader and as a human being.

George and I had very clear differences when it came to running a company. He was a real mean miserable S.O.B.—the plaque on his door said so—but I didn't invite him that day to remind him of this and say, "George, just so you know, nice guys don't finish last. Some finish first." What's the point of that? You don't need to boost yourself at someone else's expense.

I had wanted to see George again because I felt grateful for the opportunity to work for him and learn from him. And I wanted to make sure he knew this. When he hired me, he said if I went to work for him I'd learn everything about running a business—and he was right. I learned all that and more.

Luke had a somewhat similar experience to me. Where I had George, Luke had his old college golf coach. To really grow as a golfer, Luke needed a coaching style that complemented his strengths and offset his weaknesses. However, Luke's coach was very results-driven, just like Luke. That meant his coaching style reinforced some of Luke's bad habits, like being too hard on himself.

In one of our earliest lessons together, I told Luke, "I understand what happened, and I'm glad you told me, because now I know how to provide you with better direction and help. But we're never gonna complain about your old coach again. It's over. And you know what? You still learned from those four years. We're going to turn it into a positive, not a negative, going forward."

It's okay to acknowledge the hurt people may have caused you, but at a certain point, holding on to the past only hurts you. You have to let go to move forward, and finding gratitude in your experience can help. If you search for it, you'll be surprised where you can find gratitude.

EXPRESSING YOUR GRATITUDE

Aside from cultivating gratitude, expressing it is an important part of being a successful person. None of us succeeds without the many blessings we've been given. It's important to acknowledge this and express gratitude for the help we've received.

When I first started mentoring Luke, expressing gratitude—especially towards his parents—was something I worked to get him to do more often. Luke's parents are incredibly down-to-earth people, and like many parents, they want to do as much as they can for their children. They're blessed to be financially comfortable, and they've used their resources to help Luke and his six other siblings. Their support is what allowed Luke to do things like travel to golf tournaments all over the state and country. In other words, he's been blessed with great parents and great opportunities.

When you've experienced something your entire life, you don't always recognize how fortunate you are. So I challenged Luke to think more deeply about what he had to be grateful for. During one of our sessions at Chicago Golf Club, I told him, "I want you to start doing things and saying things to your mom and dad to show your appreciation. It can be little things. Maybe you decide to pick up dinner one night. Maybe you bring your mom some flowers and say, 'Mom, I really appreciate what you and dad have done for me over the last eight years of playing golf and my entire life.'"

Part of my reason for asking Luke to do this was to break down his stoic exterior and get him to show more emotion. He's a hard-driving person and hangs on tightly to his feelings. But the other part was to simply help Luke become a better person by doing something for others. When we show gratitude—when we express appreciation for the blessings and abundance we've been given—we make others feel good while making ourselves feel good.

About six weeks later, Luke's birthday rolled around, and I texted him this message:

"Happy Birthday Luke. Have fun today at
Chicago Golf Club with your dad and brothers.
I have a challenge for you today. Normally, on our birthday,
we think it's a day all about yourself. Today, I'd love
to see you work on making it about your family.
Give your mom a hug and kiss when she wishes you
Happy Birthday and thank her for being such an awesome
mom. Tell her you love her. Give your dad a hug and thank
him for all of his support and tell him you love him.
It will make them feel amazing today and you will find
tremendous satisfaction. On the course today, be happier
about your dad's and brothers' good shots than your own.
It shouldn't matter if you shoot 65 or 75, as long as your fun
quotient is high. Maybe have a game of 'Call Your Shot'

with your brothers. It will be fun and it will help each of
your games in the long run. All of these suggestions today
will help your growth in becoming the best Luke
the person. Have your best birthday ever."

Luke responded:

"Thanks for the text, Mr. Ply.
Also I love the idea and think that's very thoughtful
and would be awesome to do today.
Thanks for the idea and all your help these past six weeks.
I appreciate everything you're doing for me."

I challenged Luke to express gratitude to his family, and he
took it a step further and did me the honor of including me in his
gratitude as well. I am so proud of him for taking this mentoring
journey with me, and I've told him so.

This is one of the amazing things about gratitude: gratitude
begets gratitude. It's like a self-fulfilling prophecy. The more you
express gratitude, the more gratitude you feel. The more gratitude
you feel, the more you express it, and on and on. Not only that,
but the more you express your gratitude to others, the more they
feel gratitude too.

Luke is much happier now than when I first met him. He's laughing and having more fun on the course than before. His enjoyment level playing golf has skyrocketed! And guess what: golf hasn't changed. It's still the same game it always was. *Luke* has changed, because of gratitude. We become better people when we appreciate the abundance of our blessings and share this abundance with others.

THE ULTIMATE LEVEL OF SUCCESS: TRUE CONTENTMENT

My father would often tell me, "Johnny, I have everything. I am so happy. I love my beautiful wife. I love my children. I love my grandchildren. I love my home. There is nothing that I want. I am truly content."

That is the ultimate level of success: true contentment! I don't care who you are—whether you're a billionaire or a school teacher —you're not truly successful until you can say you're happy each and every day. We tend to think of success as striving, striving, striving towards a finish line. But there is no finish line! There is no point in life where you can say, "Okay, I'm done. I am a success now." You will experience moments of achievement, such as winning an award or getting a promotion, but these moments are fleeting. True contentment is long-lasting. It's what you feel when you get up in the morning and until you go to bed at night.

This is why I say feeling true contentment in your day-to-day life is the ultimate success.

Others might have been filled with anger and resentment after experiencing what my father did as a prisoner of war. But Ziggy's time in the prisoner camp isn't what defined him. He was defined by the person he was before, during, and after that experience. Despite the hardships, despite the horrors, despite the tragedies, he chose joy. He chose gratitude. He chose contentment.

Achieving this kind of contentment is a lifelong journey. I'm not there yet, but I'm striving for it each and every day. While gratitude isn't always easy, I remind myself of the wise words of singer-songwriter Nightbirde, who is known for her appearance on *America's Got Talent*. Nightbirde was diagnosed with breast cancer in 2017, and by 2021, when she appeared on *America's Got Talent*, the cancer had metastasized to her lungs, spine, and liver. She had been given only a 2 percent chance of survival. During her audition, she told Simon Cowell and the other judges, "You can't wait until life isn't hard anymore before you decide to be happy." Unfortunately, after a five-year battle with cancer, she passed away in 2022, at the age of thirty-one.

We have only so much time on this earth. We can't wait for the imaginary, nonexistent finish line of success to be happy. By cultivating more gratitude in our lives, we can all get closer to Ziggy's and Jane Kristen Marczewski's level of happiness, one day at a time.

CHAPTER 9

BE GENEROUS

MY SIBLINGS AND I always knew our father to be kind and generous, but there were times when the extent of his compassion for others was surprising even to us.

One of those times was when my uncle fell ill and was hospitalized for three months. Each week, my father would visit my uncle in the hospital, taking him magazines to read, food from the house, and news from the family. Anything to help pass the hours and make what must have been a lonely time for my uncle feel a little less so.

These visits would last an hour or two. But one day my dad was gone for seven to eight hours. My sister Shirley and I began to grow worried. He was in his late eighties then, and his memory was starting to slip. We thought maybe he had gotten lost or had an accident driving. I had supplied my dad with a cellphone, though he was uncomfortable using it. We had programmed the phone so he could touch one number to dial each of his five kids.

We called my dad numerous times throughout the day with no answer. Finally, late in the afternoon, my dad picked up my call.

"Dad, where've you been all day?"

"At the hospital," he said matter-of-factly.

"For seven hours?!"

He didn't seem to think that was strange at all. "Well," he explained, "over the past couple of months, when I visited your uncle, I met six other people who didn't have anybody to visit them. So, I started visiting with them. Today, I decided to spend about an hour with each one!"

He had this extraordinary capacity for empathy, my father. It was just like him. He'd see someone laid up in a hospital bed with nothing but a droning television for company and think, "No one should have to go through that alone. I bet that person could use a friend."

As he got older, my father made it a point to bring comfort and companionship to his friends and members of his community who were feeling the isolation of old age. He'd see friends from church or the senior club get placed into nursing homes. Other friends would lose a spouse and could no longer care for themselves. If you've ever cared for an elderly parent or grandparent, you know how these major life events can leave a loved one feeling very lonely and cut off. My father spent his retirement years visiting friends at their homes and care facilities, determined to bring them a small light of friendship at a time when they needed it most.

Ziggy Ply touched so many lives. This is just one of the many reasons I consider him to be the most successful person I've ever known.

SPREAD A LITTLE JOY

My brothers and sisters and I grew up poor, but we never felt poor because we were happy and we had abundant love in the family. And though we never had much money, my father taught us to be generous with what we did have. Every Sunday we went to church and as the collection basket was passed around, he always had an envelope for his church. Though we didn't have extra money to give away, my father felt it was important to teach his children to be generous and charitable. He made sure we had something to put in our small collection envelopes. My oldest brother Dave's envelope contained a quarter. My sister Mimi, as the next oldest, had a dime. Then my brother Rich and I had a nickel each in our envelopes. (My younger sister, Shirley, hadn't been born yet.)

That simple weekly act instilled generosity in me. It taught me that even when I didn't have much, I still had enough to share. I've been very blessed in life, and now I can afford to share far more. One of my favorite things to do is perform random acts of kindness for people I meet out in the world. It's a wonderful feeling to be able to brighten someone's day, even for a moment.

One time, I was at Taco Bell in Las Vegas and had my order taken by a very nice young man. It was early afternoon, not very busy, and as I was eating, I overheard the young man talking with three older women in the dining area. He was being friendly, asking these women about their day, bantering and bringing smiles to their faces. In the course of the conversation, the man mentioned that Taco Bell was his second job. His mother had recently lost her job and moved in with him, and he was working two jobs to save up for a car. He'd been saving for some time and needed just $1,000 more.

This young man's actions and story touched me, and I felt the need to help. So when he later had a free moment, I went over to talk to him. I always keep ten $100 bills in my wallet, because I never know when I might need them exactly for a moment like this. "Take this," I said, handing him $1,000.

He stared at me in complete shock.

"I thought it was really nice the way you engaged with those women, the way you chatted with them to brighten their day," I told him. "I overheard your situation. I want you to go get that car. Also, I want you to buy a book called *The Slight Edge*, and I promise someday you'll thank me more for that book than the thousand dollars."

"Are you serious?" he asked. He just couldn't believe it. When I assured him that I was indeed serious, he couldn't thank me enough. And he said, "I absolutely will go buy that book."

One thing I believe about generosity is that generosity begets more generosity. The initial act of generosity in this story wasn't mine, but that young man's. He was going through a very rough time, but he still found it within his spirit to do a small act of kindness for those women. That's why I wanted to do something for him.

When you're generous, it's also possible to impact someone's life—and the world—in ways you can't imagine. What do you think happened when that young man got home that day? He probably said to his mother, "You will not believe what happened today." His day was brightened, just how he'd brightened those women's day. Maybe my act of generosity gave him a little more hope, and perhaps *The Slight Edge* proved useful to him. Maybe his kindness towards those women inspired one of them, or all of them, to find a way to help others and carry the feeling of kindness and generosity forward. This is why it's important to be generous. It is a way of multiplying goodness in the world. When someone is the recipient of kindness and generosity, they tend to be kinder and more generous to those around them.

More than anything, generosity is a way for us to connect with others. A single kind conversation might not be life-changing, and $1,000 didn't solve all of this young man's problems. But by giving his time and attention, the young man brought those women unexpected joy, and my gift told him he was seen and appreciated. Life can be hard and lonely. We all have times when we could use a little help, and you never know how much a small moment of kindness and support could mean to someone.

A GENEROSITY OF TIME AND SPIRIT

When we think about generosity, our minds typically go straight to money. If you have money to spare, then by all means be generous with it. Generosity, however, is about so much more than just money. The most valuable thing we all can give of ourselves is our time and our spirit.

My father's spirit is what he shared with the strangers he visited in the hospital. Money wouldn't have done anything for them. What he gave them was far more meaningful. He provided fellowship and the warmth of human connection. Time is what he gave to his church, Saint Phillip's, where he was an usher for thirty years. Except if he was sick, my father never missed a service. Every single parishioner knew Ziggy Ply. He was so proud to do that job, and it really was a job, one he did for free.

My parents were generous in the love and affection they gave to us children. We didn't get away with anything. Punishment and discipline (like the time my brother and I were caught stealing from Dad's coin collection) was always stern and swift, but followed up with a reminder of how much they loved us. After long, stressful, exhausting days, they still always made time for us.

Sure, we can all appreciate money, but often it's generosity of time and spirit that makes the biggest impact on people. Not long ago, Luke and his family went on vacation together. It's a big family. There are seven kids, several of whom have their own children now. Luke's father sent me a short video clip of the whole family, captioned, "Luke holding court telling the family about John Ply." At that point, Luke and I had only been working together six, maybe seven weeks. His father then told me, "If you never spoke to Luke again, you have done more for him than you will ever know. He is happy again. We have our son back. You made a difference in his/our life. Money can't buy that."

This is what generosity is about. You don't have to be rich to make a difference in people's lives. Ultimately, generosity is what you give of yourself to others. It's about caring for others and sharing your time and spirit. True success is being able to look back on your life and recognize that life is not measured by material possessions or the money you've accumulated, but by the joy you've brought to others. If you can do good for just one person, then you should consider that a success.

HOW TO BE MORE GENEROUS

I've met people who are ten times wealthier than me, and for whatever reason, they're not generous. They've created great wealth —they've been fortunate enough to have done that—but then they don't do much good with it. What's the purpose in that?

How many cars, how many houses, how many of anything do you really need? I know people who have a dozen or more golf club memberships, which seems quite excessive to me. It's impossible to enjoy a dozen golf memberships. They're paying membership dues and fees at each club when they could be doing so much more with that money to help others.

To be more generous, the first step is to recognize that you have enough—more than enough actually, which means you have enough to give. It might not be money, but there's something you have that you can share.

Then you look for places where there's a need. For example, I'm constantly looking for charitable organizations that get overlooked. There are many well-deserving groups that have great needs that don't pop up on everyone's radar. I'm more interested in helping these groups because the impact of your contribution often goes much further. In business speak, the return on investment is greater.

Again, it doesn't have to be money. Donating your time and skills can have a great impact. You have skills you can contribute, whether you're great at marketing, writing, fundraising, organizing, etc. My best friend Jack (the one who suggested I become a caddie and who wrote the foreword), started teaching advanced algebra to seventh- and eighth-graders after his first retirement from his banking career. He has done this for twenty-one straight years now, for free! I admire him so very much! He goes above and beyond to try to make math fun for the kids. Once a year, Jack invites me as a guest teacher for his eighth-grade class to help them understand how they'll use what they are learning throughout their lives. I bring a case of gourmet hot chocolate, and Jack and I task the kids with calculating the total cost to manufacture the case, based on the number of packets in a case, the weight of each packet, the percentage and cost of each ingredient, the cost of the packaging materials, the cost to blend powder, and the unit cost to fill each packet. I always reward the first three students who come up with the correct answer, typically with a Susan B. Anthony dollar coin or a two-dollar bill. None of the kids go home empty-handed, though, because I always bring enough hot cocoa so each student can go home with a dozen packets.

Jack told me that one year, after my visit, a student took note of my leather jacket and nice watch and asked, "Is Mr. Ply rich?" The question was somewhat unusual, but Jack used it as a teaching opportunity. He told the students he'd known me his whole life. I had in fact grown up poor, but I worked hard and applied what I learned in school to start a successful business with just a single mixer. "If you guys work hard and study hard, and continue to learn from others," he said, "you, too, can be just like Mr. Ply someday." So I guess my visits are actually more than just about algebra! The idea is to impress upon the students that what they're learning at school, which can sometimes seem meaningless and even boring, is something they can and will use out in the real world.

You use what you have to make a difference—your time, your resources, your skills. For my friend Jack, it's been teaching. For me, it's been sharing life lessons and mentoring. Though I sold Insight Beverages in 2015, Jack still invites me to his class to give his students a real-life example of what he teaches them every day. It's a tradition we both look forward to.

One thing everyone has is the capacity for empathy, the ability to let others know they are not alone. You can be the friendly voice on the line, or the helping hand at someone's doorstep. Oftentimes, the greatest service we can provide another is to let them know there is no burden they need to shoulder alone. The other day, I called up a friend I hadn't spoken with in a long while. At the end of the call, he said, "God, I really needed a John Ply fix today." Let me tell you, his comment made me feel like a million bucks. I had never thought of our conversations that way, as an injection of happiness and positivity. All I had given him was time and a listening ear. At the time, I didn't even think of it as being generous, but that's apparently what it was.

We can all do something for someone else, regardless of our circumstances. There are so many opportunities to show kindness and generosity towards others simply as we go about our daily lives. It can be giving up your seat on the bus or train, or giving up your place in line. It can be as easy as saying to someone on the elevator, "How's your day going? I hope you have a good day." Instead of looking at your phone and avoiding eye contact, looking up to acknowledge someone can be a powerful way to make someone's day a little brighter.

When you do something kind for someone else, it can have a tremendous impact. It makes you feel really good, and at the same time, they might feel, "Gosh, maybe life is okay. Maybe things are going to be okay after all."

A GENEROUS SOUL WILL PROSPER

When I gave the eulogy for my father's funeral, I spoke about his kindness and generosity. I saw many in attendance nodding in affirmation as they remembered what my father had done for them or their fathers, mothers, uncles, aunts, and spouses. There wasn't a dry eye in the church.

Generosity is first and foremost about what you give, but the truth is that when you give, you also receive. My father had so many incredible relationships and received so much love because he was generous with everything that he had.

Giving to others sets up a world in which others give to you. While we all have things we can give, we all also have things we could stand to receive, even if we don't realize it. As an example, I was practicing golf with a friend of mine, Alan Battersby. He mentioned that he really liked this training aid I use to correct the flaws in my swing. I was pretty sure I had another one at home, so I gave him mine. Alan asked me what he owed me for it. "Nothing," I said. "It's a gift."

Not long after, Alan returned the favor by giving me a copy of his brother's book. The book? *The Golf Mystic* by Gary Battersby! That book has been invaluable to me. I've learned so much from it, and I've shared it with many others. Through exploring the book's lessons, I was also able to meet Gary and form a friendship that has enlarged my understanding of life.

And this was all due to a moment of serendipity when I parted with a small material possession and expected nothing in return. The universe works in funny ways. I might have never discovered *The Golf Mystic* had I not taken the opportunity to be generous with a friend.

If you are generous, you will be rewarded. There's no telling what the reward might be—a gift, a word of thanks, an introduction to something new you didn't know you needed, or simply the feeling of satisfaction and fulfillment that comes from making an impact. Whatever the case may be, being generous to others can only turn into something good. And I believe "to do good" is truly our only purpose in life!

CHAPTER 10

DO GOOD

MY FATHER ZIGGY never did nice things for himself. If he had spare money or time, he was going to spend it on others, not himself. That was more rewarding to him.

Finally, at the age of forty-five, he did one nice thing for himself. After living in America for sixteen years, my father treated himself to an airline ticket to Poland.

This was in 1966. I was eleven years old. My father had last set foot on Polish soil in 1939, when the Germans captured him, and he hadn't seen his family since 1937, when he joined the Polish army. Nearly three decades separated my father and his Polish family. During that time, my father had married and was raising five kids in America. Meanwhile, his parents had grown old, and his siblings were raising families of their own. You can imagine the joy, excitement, and trepidation he must have felt preparing for this momentous reunion.

My father's trip lasted two weeks. It was the longest time he and my mother had been apart. In their fourteen years of marriage up to that point, they'd never spent even a day apart. They wrote each other love notes, and my mother planned a big party for his return. I remember the colorful streamers and signs she put up around the house: "Welcome Home, Honey!" and "Welcome Back, Daddy!"

After two weeks, my father came into the house, exhausted but elated and somehow missing the suitcase he'd departed with. He came back with just the clothes on his body. This wasn't due to an airline mix-up. Everything he'd carried onto the plane two weeks earlier had been purposely left behind in Poland. As little as my dad had, his relatives had even less, so he gave them everything. His extra clothes and shoes, his coat, his shaving kit, his toothbrush and toothpaste, his suitcase itself, everything.

He was afraid my mother would be mad at him. But she wasn't. Instead, she was proud.

That's just who Ziggy was. If he had a chance to do good, he did it.

OPERATION: CARE PACKAGE

That trip triggered something in my father. Every year over the next approximately forty-five years, he sent hundreds of parcels to family members in Poland, probably well over a thousand care packages in total. He sent items that many Americans would take for granted but were difficult to obtain in a Communist country.

He would shop the Blue Light Specials at Kmart and hunt through Walmart for bargains so he could stock up. He bought shoes, bras, underwear, clothes, deodorant, toothpaste, toothbrushes, Lipton tea bags, hot chocolate, macaroni and cheese, and other staple food items. Boxes and boxes of stuff to make life in an impoverished country a little easier. Hard currency was something his relatives needed, and though my father didn't have much, he often slipped in a $5 or $10 or $20 bill.

My father retired from meatpacking in 1985, and he spent his retirement years and income taking care of others in Poland. His operation grew with time. He found a company to help facilitate the flow of boxes through Polish customs. He kept meticulous notebooks that documented everything that went over. He knew boxes would take three weeks to arrive, and he staggered shipments to keep the flow constant. After sending a batch of boxes over, he'd immediately start filling his next shipment.

Throughout the 1980s and early 1990s, my father supported his care package operation solely on his retirement income. Helping people is what he did, and he always gave to people who had less than himself. Then in late 1993 I started my second company, Pinnacle Food Products. Within five years it was enjoying considerable success, and I was able to repay the tremendous debt I owed my dad in a really big way.

Many of the boxes my father shipped contained nonperishables, and that's something Pinnacle Food Products specialized in. One of our top sellers was this wonderful gourmet hot chocolate. I gave him cases and cases of it to send over. Poland can get pretty cold in the winters, so the people loved it over there. I also gave him cases of instant soup and a line of instant products called Mexi Magic, which included nacho cheese mix, jalapeno bean dip, French onion dip, and ranch party dip. I suppose I'm biased, but those dips were delicious—way better than any dip you could buy in the store. My friends were always asking me to send them more Mexi Magic. And these dips were so easy to make! All you had to do was add water to the powders, which made them perfect to send to Poland, where, at the time, many ingredients normally found in dips (like sour cream) were difficult or even impossible to find.

Once Pinnacle Food Products hit its stride, I was able to support my father in a more significant way. My brother Rich had gone over to Poland to visit our father's family and explore his roots. When he came back, he said, "John, these people are in really rough shape. I think you could make a real difference there."

"How much money do you think it would take?" I asked. My brother thought $250,000 would get the job done.

With my dad's quite large number of relatives, it took a bit more than that. In the ten years between 1998 and 2008, I ended up giving my father $1 million to distribute to his sixty-seven family members. The money went to his brothers and sisters and their kids and grandkids, people who were my uncles and aunts, cousins, and cousins' children. So many people my father was able to help. After his initial trip in 1966, he was sending $10 and $20 at a time. Now, he was wiring $10,000 and $20,000 at a time, usually around the major holidays during the year, to be split among all this family.

The money lifted them out of poverty. They were able to buy better clothes and move into better apartments. At the time, $2,000 bought a small car in Poland, which enabled them to drive to work, making their commute easier and faster. It was a great way for me to give back to my father for loaning me nearly all of his savings to help my business. He cried many times from the joy he felt from being able to help his family in such a big way.

The last time he went back to Poland to visit, all sixty-seven relatives welcomed him at the airport with flowers and hugs and kisses. He was in his eighties by then, and he was just beside himself that he could help and make a difference in their lives.

THE ANSWER TO EVERYTHING: TO DO GOOD

My father made it his life's purpose to do good for others, and it took me a long time to understand this was my purpose as well.

Around the time I turned forty years old, I was feeling uneasy and wasn't as happy as I probably should have been. There was the stress of running two companies, and even with the financial benefits of Pinnacle Food Products beginning to do well, I was struggling mentally. We were in the third year of Pinnacle Food Products and really gaining traction. After zero dollars in sales the first year and only $220,000 in sales our second year, we had a fabulous jump to $1.8 million in sales the third year.

When you're the head of two companies that employ a couple hundred people, there's no one you can really share or talk with. Every day I struggled with the question, "Why am I not feeling as happy as I should?" My two sons were doing great, and going to their games and doing stuff with them brought me joy. But most days I struggled. There was something missing, and I didn't know what it was.

I turned introspective. I asked myself, "What is my purpose? What am I doing here? Was I put on this earth to blend and package powdered food products?"

I don't think so, I thought to myself. *There's got to be more.* And that's when it came to me. I don't know how the thought was triggered, but my mind narrowed in on this: we were put on this earth for only one reason—to do good.

That's the answer, to success, to life, to happiness, to everything. To do good. There was something about those words that really hit me hard. We weren't put on this earth to hurt people or steal and cheat and kill. We were put on this earth to do good—to help others when we can and leave the world a better place than we found it.

Ever since that day, that's what I've tried to do. I credit my father for helping me reach this point. He was sending care packages to Poland and visiting with his aging friends, and I could see how much helping others lifted his spirits, and I learned from his example.

There's something inherently good about being good. Not only do you make other people feel good, you make yourself feel good. It's a double dose of goodness. And it's never artificial if it's true goodness. You do it because you mean what you're doing and you mean what you say.

Over the past few decades, "to do good" has become my guiding light. Each and every day, I work to be a better person and look for opportunities to do good for others around me—be it family, friends, or a complete stranger. "To do good" changed my whole perspective. By making this one small shift in mindset, I was able to approach every day with positivity, and approach everyone in a way that spreads happiness and kindness.

My father was deeply religious, and though I am not a big churchgoer myself, I am guided by faith and a belief that a higher power gave us skills to use in the service of doing good for others. Nine times out of ten, the opportunities come in daily interactions and being kind to the people around you. Maybe it's starting a conversation with a stranger, helping someone out in the checkout line who's short a couple of bucks, or doing a random act of kindness. You can do good simply by being aware of the people around you. It doesn't cost anything to hold the door open for the person behind you, to say hello to someone in the elevator, or to acknowledge someone with a smile.

There are hundreds and hundreds of ways to do good. You can give your time. You can be charitable. You can be a listening ear. All it means to do good is to give of yourself without looking for something in return.

As I said earlier, financial wealth does not buy happiness. It only buys comfort. You buy happiness with acts of goodness. My father lived that way, and he was the happiest person I ever knew. Imagine what the world would be like if we all lived by his example.

PAY IT FORWARD

Doing good is rewarding in and of itself, but I also think it's our duty, because none of us make it through life without receiving help.

My parents helped me by paying my first semester at Fenwick High School, and when I needed a loan to start Priority Food Processing, they dipped into most of their savings. Their financial sacrifice for me not only gave me the means to start my first company, but also instilled a confidence in my belief that I could build a great company. Although I replenished their savings, paid for medications and other things they needed when they got older, and helped our relatives back in Poland, none of this could truly pay my parents back.

There were other mentor-type people who helped me along the way, people such as John Gleason Sr. (Jack Gleason's father) and John O'Neill Sr. I could never repay them for the help they gave me and the examples they set on how to treat others.

That leaves only one option: I need to pay it forward.

This is why I approached Lilia Vu that day on the driving range. It's why I mentor young people like Luke after he finished playing college golf and Jeff as he contemplated a career as a Navy Seal. I could never repay the debt to my elders who helped me when I was young, but I can lend a hand and an attentive ear to those just starting in their life when they are likely to need it most.

In a way, mentoring younger people is something I've always done, though I didn't think of it as mentoring at the time. John O'Neill Sr. was someone I knew through his son, John Jr. John Jr. and I met at Oak Park Country Club when he was twelve and I was fifteen. I took John Jr. under my wing, offering advice about caddying and our love of golf. Our friendship has been lifelong, and it's enriched us both.

Like his father, John O'Neill Jr. is a great man and yet he thinks of me as his mentor. Recently, he sent me the most stunning letter that left tears in my eyes: "Since I was the oldest boy in my family, I didn't have an older brother," his letter said. "You probably didn't know it, but you filled that role for me. You offered advice about caddying, golf, Fenwick, family, college, and much more. You were living your mantra, 'to do good,' long before it was your mantra. My life has been greatly enhanced by your presence, my friend."

When you do good for others, you do good for yourself. It brings me so much joy and satisfaction to watch young people become who they are and reach their full potential. One of the nicest compliments I ever received was when Lilia's mother told me at lunch one day earlier this year that it was truly a gift from God that I happened to be next to her daughter on the range that day! I'm certain I also received a gift that same day. In an interview where she talked about turning around her career, Lilia referred to me as the "man at the range," and I absolutely loved that. I feel so much joy every time I watch Lilia Vu play, and I sincerely believe she will reach her ultimate goal of becoming the best. She finished her first season back on the LPGA with eight top-ten finishes, coming in thirtieth on the money list, with $918,939. With a current ranking of number forty-one in the world, she is well on her way to becoming number one! I would love to see her become the face of the LPGA, not for her sake, but for all the young golfers out there. She's the kind of person the LPGA will love having as a representative of the Tour. No matter where she's at on the leaderboard, she exudes graciousness and appreciation for her success. She's so articulate, and she shows kindness to her fellow competitors and fans of the game. I know she will pay it forward when her time comes.

When you pay it forward, you become a link in an unbroken chain dating all the way back to humanity's start. It's the greatest tradition of our species: people helping people. This is the thing that sets us apart from all other life on earth. Someone helped you, so you help others, and they will help yet more people in the future, and on and on. I'm proud of the ways I've helped people like Lilia, Luke, Jeff, Alfonso, and John Jr., but I'm even more proud of what they have accomplished and will go on to accomplish. I know they will do more good and positively impact other lives throughout the rest of theirs!

A GENEROUS SPIRIT, A CONTAGIOUS SMILE

My father lived to be ninety-four years old. I have no doubt he was with us for so long because of the good he brought to others. He was a beacon of happiness and positivity, and he was the kind of man I think we don't see very often. He just brought happiness to whomever needed it.

I think about him visiting those strangers in the hospital when my uncle fell ill, and I think about him checking in with his aging friends at their homes and care facilities. At ninety-two years old, Ziggy Ply was still ushering at his church on Sundays, greeting people with a generous spirit and infectious smile. People like my father bring something much needed to the world. I'm glad for the time we had with him, and I know many others were glad too.

When you spend a life doing good like Ziggy, you don't leave this world when you die. You leave behind fingerprints, traces of impact. When my son Zach got married, I gifted him a watch. On the backplate are my initials, his initials, and space for his son's initials, and inscribed in the center are the words "To do good." That's a piece of Ziggy right there, a legacy he passed on to me, that I've passed on to my sons, who will pass it on to their children.

It is my hope these words will guide many generations of Plys to come—and you too. In that way, the memory of my father will live forever.

CONCLUSION

People often used to joke about my father being a saint. Everyone did! My mom joked about it. My siblings and I did. His grandkids did. Even our neighbors joked about it.

Looking back on his life and what he did, he *was* a saint. He was put on this earth to make people happier. Anyone he touched, he brought joy to their day, and that's what a saint would do.

Who would wander into a hospital room and chat with strangers because they had no one visiting them? Who would find the equivalent of two weeks' wages on the ground and attempt to locate its owner? Who would single-handedly care for his wife while also visiting nursing homes to offer friends and acquaintances a dose of human connection against the solitude of old age? Who would send package after package to distant relatives in Poland to help ease their lives?

Kind of saint-like, don't you think?

I try to do good, but I can't hold a candle to my father. He set an incredible example for me. I can honestly say his example has driven me to become the person who I am today. Now, there's no way I can become Ziggy Ply. None of us can. He's untouchable.

But we can at least try to become like him, to get somewhere close. And if we do, we'll actually achieve a lot in life, both personally and professionally.

Chicago Golf Club has a motto: Far and Sure. It's good advice for golf and life. Aim far, dreaming as big as you can. Then go after it with surety—with confidence and faith that you can do it. That's what it means to be like Ziggy. Give your all and try your hardest, no matter the task. Pursue your passion, and use all the tools at your disposal to achieve your goals. Never give up, and if you encounter an obstacle, find a way. Be honest with others, and be open and trusting. Offer your kindness and generosity of spirit to your friends, your family, and that stranger ahead of you in the checkout line. Instead of complaining, be grateful for your blessings. Do good for others, and multiply the goodness in the world.

I made you a big promise at the start of this book. I told you that you can be the best. I truly believe that, and I hope by now you believe it too. Because the thing about that promise is that I'm not the one who can keep it. You are. I've shared the lessons with you, and now it's up to you to put them into practice.

Let me share one final secret about golf and life with you. No one ever really masters golf; people just get better than others at it. The same goes for life. You never conquer life. You just learn from your experiences and try to do a little better—to be a little more like Ziggy—than the day before. Your journey may be long, with ups and downs, and it won't always be easy. It will require faith and belief in yourself, and your work will never be done.

But you can do it. One day at a time, far and sure, *you can be the best!*

ACKNOWLEDGMENTS

I am forever grateful for the talent, creativity, and the belief of Kelsey Adams. Kelsey's expertise as a writer made my ideas and experiences come to life in a way I could never have created on my own. Her belief in the possibilities of this book saved it from a time I truly thought it might need to be forgotten.

My deepest thanks go out to Lilia Vu, Luke, Jeff, Alfonso, and John O'Neill Jr. for their trust and belief in allowing me to be a small part of their lives and journeys. I will cherish our times together and their friendships forever.

Words cannot describe what it's like to have a lifelong friend like Jack Gleason and to have him write such a humbling foreword to this endeavor.

Heartfelt thanks to my sister Mimi, for helping me properly and accurately share our father's inspiring life journey and his deep love for our mother, his children, and so many other lives he touched in a way only Ziggy could do.

Lastly, loving thanks to my beautiful wife, Cynthia, for always showing her support for what at times seemed to be an all-consuming project.

CPSIA information can be obtained
at www.ICGtesting.com
Printed in the USA
JSHW080540040423
39852JS00003B/5/J